COMMERCIAL FISHING IN ALASKA

BY JOEL GAY

ALASKA GEOGRAPHIC®   VOLUME 24, NUMBER 3

To teach many more to better know and more wisely use our natiural resources...

EDITOR
Penny Rennick

PRODUCTION DIRECTOR
Kathy Doogan

MARKETING MANAGER
Pattey Parker Mancini

CIRCULATION/DATABASE MANAGER
Linda Flowers

EDITORIAL ASSISTANT
Kerre Martineau

BOARD OF DIRECTORS
Richard Carlson
Kathy Doogan
Penny Rennick

Robert A. Henning, **PRESIDENT EMERITUS**

POSTMASTER: Send address changes to:

ALASKA GEOGRAPHIC®
P.O. Box 93370
Anchorage, Alaska 99509-3370

PRINTED IN U.S.A.

ISBN: 1-56661-035-4

PRICE TO NON-MEMBERS THIS ISSUE: $19.95

ALASKA GEOGRAPHIC® (ISSN 0361-1353) is published quarterly by The Alaska Geographic Society, 639 W. International Airport Rd., Unit 38, Anchorage, AK 99518. Periodicals postage paid at Anchorage, Alaska, and additional mailing offices. Copyright © 1997 by The Alaska Geographic Society. All rights reserved. Registered trademark: Alaska Geographic, ISSN 0361-1353; Key title Alaska Geographic.

THE ALASKA GEOGRAPHIC SOCIETY is a non-profit, educational organization dedicated to improving geographic understanding of Alaska and the North, putting geography back in the classroom and exploring new methods of teaching and learning.

MEMBERS RECEIVE *ALASKA GEOGRAPHIC®*, a high-quality, colorful quarterly that devotes each issue to monographic, in-depth coverage of a northern region or resource-oriented subject. Back issues are also available. For current membership rates, or to order or request a free catalog of back issues, contact: Alaska Geographic Society, P.O. Box 93370, Anchorage, AK 99509-3370; phone (907) 562-0164, fax (907) 562-0479, e-mail: akgeo@aol.com.

SUBMITTING PHOTOGRAPHS: Those interested in submitting photographs for possible publication should write for a list of upcoming topics or other specific photo needs and a copy of our editorial guidelines. We cannot be responsible for unsolicited submissions. Submissions not accompanied by sufficient postage for return by certified mail will be returned by regular mail.

CHANGE OF ADDRESS: The post office will not automatically forward *ALASKA GEOGRAPHIC®* when you move. To ensure continuous service, please notify us at least six weeks before moving. Send your new address and membership number or a mailing label from a recent issue of *ALASKA GEOGRAPHIC®* to: Alaska Geographic Society, Box 93370, Anchorage, AK 99509. If your book is returned to us by the post office because of an incorrect address, we will contact you to ask if you wish to receive a replacement book for $5 (this fee covers additional postage costs only).

COLOR SEPARATIONS: Graphic Chromatics

PRINTING: Hart Press

The Library of Congress has cataloged this serial publication as follows:

Alaska Geographic. v.1-
   [Anchorage, Alaska Geographic Society] 1972-
   v. ill. (part col.). 23 x 31 cm.
   Quarterly
   Official publication of The Alaska Geographic Society.
   Key title: Alaska geographic, ISSN 0361-1353.

   1. Alaska—Description and travel—1959-
   —Periodicals. I. Alaska Geographic Society.

F901.A266 917.98'04'505 72-92087

Library of Congress 75[79112] MARC-S.

COVER: *Fishermen battle for position at the North Line during Bristol Bay's valuable sockeye salmon fishery.* (Art Sutch)

PREVIOUS PAGE: *Albert Howard indicates thumbs up amid a deck full of pink salmon aboard a fishing vessel in Chatham Strait.* (Ed LeDoux)

FACING PAGE: *A crew member signals the skipper operating the hydraulics to open the zipper on a net full of pollock on the* Ocean Hope 3 *trawler out of Kodiak.* (Daryl Binney)

ABOUT THIS ISSUE: Joel Gay wrote *Commercial Fishing in Alaska*, with the exception of "Observing: The Future of the Seas," written by Daryl Binney. Joel has lived in Homer since 1976 and written about Alaska's commercial fishing industry since 1980 for the *Homer News*, *National Fisherman*, *Pacific Fishing* and other magazines and newspapers. He has fished commercially for salmon and herring, operated a salmon tender and is currently managing editor of the *Homer News*. Daryl, a 10-year resident of Alaska and originally from New York state, has a biological science degree from Syracuse University and a photography degree from Montana State. She was in the Peace Corps in Burkina Faso, Africa.

CONTENTS

INTRODUCTION

Dawn was a thin band of orange under a broad, gray sky on my first day of commercial salmon fishing in Alaska, a June morning cold enough to see my breath. The hills of Kamishak Bay were still brown and the beaches had yet to lose all their snow. I climbed to the crow's nest to hand the skipper a bowl of hot oatmeal as we motored quietly around the shallow waters of Mikfik Lagoon, looking for the telltale sign that Alaska fishermen have always sought — jumpers.

No one knows why salmon leap. Poets say it's out of joy, pragmatists say navigation. When I saw my first, I yelped and quickly pointed, certain the skipper would be pleased.

"Don't point!" he hissed. Some other boat might see, and steal "our" fish.

We were hunters, I soon came to realize, quietly cruising this tiny bay in hopes of cashing in on its natural bounty. Our net and boat were improvements over the tools of our Alaska Native forebears, and the currency of exchange was different, but in essence we were doing the same thing — trying to put away as much fish as we could before the salmon run expired for another year. Like them, we got up early and worked into the thin twilight of Alaska's summer. If another boat had broken down or needed salt or bread, we wouldn't hesitate to help. But when the fish were in the lagoon, it was every tiny tribe for itself.

Though they all share the thrill of the chase, it would be a stretch to call commercial fishermen on the eve of the 21st century the last of the hunter-gatherers. The range of Alaska fisheries is so broad that "fisherman" describes tens of thousands of individuals, from gruff old bachelors in open skiffs who may indeed be fishing for that night's dinner to the captains of 350-foot floating cities that catch, process and freeze their prey and remain at sea for months at a time. Together they catch some 6 billion pounds of fish a year valued at $2 billion, making commercial fishing the second biggest industry in Alaska.

The majority of fishermen, however, work on small boats in coastal waters. They might fish for salmon, crab, shrimp, halibut, herring or cod. Most fish part of the year for a few species, often with their spouses or children on board. Some fishermen are women, some are teen-agers, many are Alaska Natives and a few are immigrants. They are the quintessential small businessmen, turning a

FACING PAGE: *Kodiak, with St. Paul Harbor above and St. Herman's Harbor below, is second only to Dutch Harbor among Alaska fishing ports. (Tom Culkin)*

The President Polk, *one of the American President Lines vessels, carries Alaska seafood to Asia from Dutch Harbor. High-priority cargo such as seafood is put into 40-foot refrigerated containers for shipment. (Dan Parrett)*

natural resource into family income. A number have become wealthy, others have died at sea, but most "just fish," taking in stride the resource's seasonal nature and the cycles of supply and demand.

At times fishing was the hardest work I have ever done, as well as the dumbest. Twenty-hour days are typical, though sometimes sleep is impossible even then because the wrists or fingers ache so badly from pulling in nets and picking fish. Once, after an already-long day, our boat went dry on a Bristol Bay beach with the net still out and full of fish. Fearing we would waste three tons of sockeyes unless we got them into our hold, each of us carried a ton of fish back to the boat, six at a time. I could hardly pitch the last few from the beach up to the deck, and couldn't pick up the coffee pot the next morning.

Alaska is rife with myths about rich fishermen but whatever I earned that day was not enough. I recall 24-hour periods in which I made an easy $1,000, as well as a month that netted just $300. Other fishermen have pocketed far more and far less depending on their skill, nerve and luck, like the friends who caught nearly $300,000 worth of herring in 20 minutes. The crew took home almost $30,000 apiece.

The business has rewards other than money, however. Working along the state's 10,000 miles of coastline can be likened to a floating camping trip in a 32-foot aluminum tent. I've watched the golden shoulder hump of a brown bear ripple as the bear swam near us off Kodiak. Otters have slithered down the banks of a beach in Port Dick as we fished nearby. Humpback whales "spy-hopped" high into the air all around us near Togiak and Dall's porpoises leapt out of the water near Gore Point. Bristol Bay has yielded morning skies the color of tangerines and peaches and wisps of fog lovingly draped on coastal bluffs.

The joy of fishing often comes from the simplest things. A dry pair of rubber gloves or a fresh tomato are precious gifts after a month at sea. Even a storm can be a welcome event, bringing a day of deep sleep in a

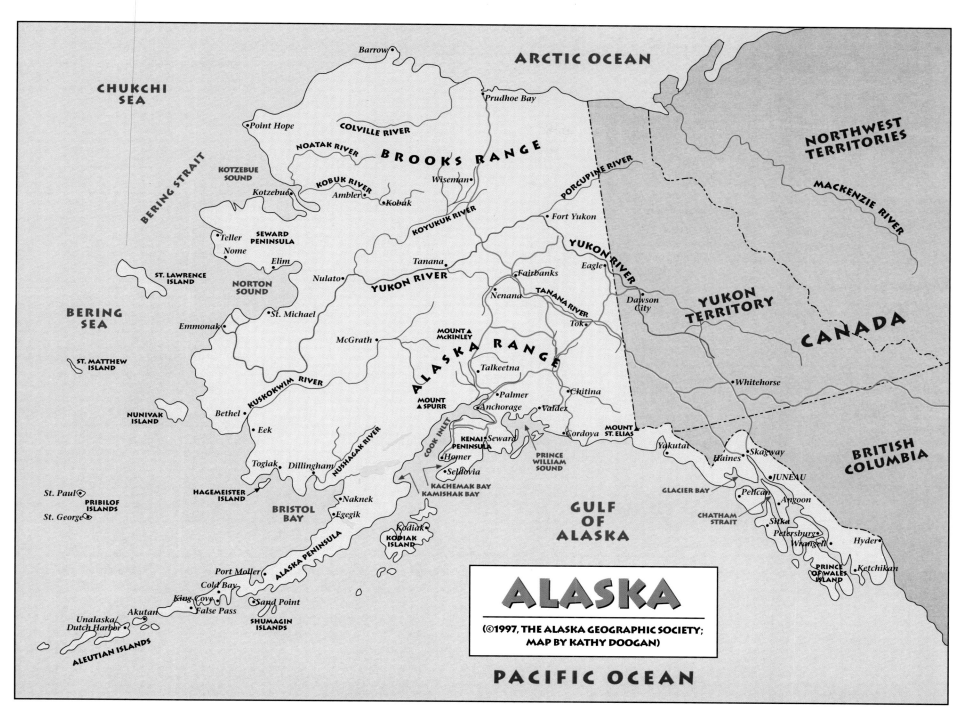

CHUKCHI SEA

ARCTIC OCEAN

Barrow

Prudhoe Bay

Point Hope

COLVILLE RIVER

NOATAK RIVER

BROOKS RANGE

NORTHWEST TERRITORIES

MACKENZIE RIVER

KOTZEBUE SOUND

KOBUK RIVER

Wiseman

BERING STRAIT

Kotzebue *Ambler* *Kobuk*

PORCUPINE RIVER

KOYUKUK RIVER

Fort Yukon

Teller

SEWARD PENINSULA

Nome

Elim

Tanana

Fairbanks

Eagle

YUKON RIVER

ST. LAWRENCE ISLAND

NORTON SOUND

Nulato

YUKON RIVER

Nenana

TANANA RIVER

Dawson City

YUKON TERRITORY

BERING SEA

St. Michael

Tok

CANADA

Emmonak

McGrath

MOUNT McKINLEY ▲

ALASKA RANGE

ST. MATTHEW ISLAND

Talkeetna

Chitina

Whitehorse

KUSKOKWIM RIVER

MOUNT ▲ SPURR

Palmer

NUNIVAK ISLAND

Bethel

Eek

Anchorage

Valdez

Cordova

MOUNT ST. ELIAS

Yakutat

Haines *Skagway*

BRITISH COLUMBIA

NUSHAGAK RIVER

COOK INLET

KENAI PENINSULA

Seward

PRINCE WILLIAM SOUND

GLACIER BAY

JUNEAU

Togiak *Dillingham*

Homer

Seldovia

Pelican

Angoon

St. Paul

PRIBILOF ISLANDS

HAGEMEISTER ISLAND

Naknek

KACHEMAK BAY
KAMISHAK BAY

GULF OF ALASKA

CHATHAM STRAIT

Sitka

St. George

BRISTOL BAY

Egegik

Petersburg

Wrangell

Hyder

Kodiak

KODIAK ISLAND

Port Moller

ALASKA PENINSULA

PRINCE OF WALES ISLAND

Ketchikan

Cold Bay

King Cove

Sand Point

Akutan *False Pass*

SHUMAGIN ISLANDS

Unalaska/ Dutch Harbor

ALEUTIAN ISLANDS

ALASKA

(©1997, THE ALASKA GEOGRAPHIC SOCIETY; MAP BY KATHY DOOGAN)

PACIFIC OCEAN

gently rocking bunk. One of my most memorable nights was spent listening to 50-knot gusts shriek overhead and nursing cups of tea as the crew slept and the orange flame of the oil stove danced quietly on the cabin walls.

Still, it always seems too early when the skipper grinds the diesel engine back to life. The first cup of coffee has little effect and the wrists soon throb as if yesterday were still not done. A waffle with whipped cream would be a delight, but generic Cheerios and boxed milk will have to do. Fish, deliver, sleep, eat. Day turns into night, then day, and night, and soon all that matters is the tide.

When people work long hours in stressful conditions, their worst sides often come out. So can their best. Boats I've been on have foregone good fishing to help out stranded friends and pitched in to aid complete strangers. We've shared information with fishery managers that reduced our catch and at times demanded that areas be closed for conservation. When fishing was good, we've called our friends, and called them, too, when it was bad. Skippers who compete fiercely on the grounds often as not share a laugh when the season is over, chalking up their previous hostility to the urgency of the situation.

For nearly a decade after that first fishing trip I spent every spring or summer on a fishing boat, as a deck hand and then as a skipper, and my heart still quickens every time I see a boat under way. Part of me longs to be on deck, with the wind in my face and the sea beneath my feet. I also recall the long days and the worry, and usually am glad to be watching from shore.

To this day, however, my hands stay in my pockets and I point with eyes and chin when I murmur, "Jumper, one o'clock."◄

FACING PAGE: *Several types of fishing industry vessels from small catcher boats to a large freighter line up near Togiak during the herring fishery. (Greg Syverson)*

RIGHT: *A good load of sockeye salmon brings a look of satisfaction to these crew members as they wait at the tender to unload their catch. (Art Sutch)*

SALMON

The season was just half an hour old when Mike said, "OK, let's see what we've got."

As he ran the hydraulics and spooled the net onto the reel, his son Louie and I watched excitedly — I more than he. Louie was 16, a veteran of eight seasons in Bristol Bay and already bored. This was my first.

We knew we had fish. As soon as the net stretched out in the water they began to hit, each kicking up a little death-dance geyser like someone had left the lid off a blender of Margaritas. Now we would find out how many.

The first few sockeyes emerged from the olive-green water listless; Mike and Louie wrestled them out of the net and pitched them into the hold. But when a live one came across the stern roller, Mike extracted it carefully — and kissed it. A big smooch right on the lips. Then he held it up to me. "Gotta kiss the first fish," he said, with a smile but dead serious. "It's good luck." He had fished in Alaska for 20 seasons and it was apparent this was protocol. So I kissed it, too. After a brief, teen-age rebellion summarily quashed by his father, Louie followed suit.

"He's just gonna get caught by someone else," the son said half-heartedly as the salmon splashed back into the water, got its bearings and disappeared. "Maybe so," replied the father. "Maybe so."

If there is a single fish synonymous with Alaska's commercial fisheries, it is the salmon. Powerful, beautiful and valuable, salmon epitomize the bounty of nature and the hardy North Pacific. The ways of the world seem embodied in the species' life history, from the mysterious appearance of the hatchlings out of the river gravel and their downstream journey to the big unknown to their inevitable return a year or more later and ritualistic mating, spawning and death. At once the fish are concrete and magical, temporal and enduring, of the earth and heavenly.

The aboriginal peoples of the Pacific Rim have revered the salmon since the ice receded some 10,000 years ago, and the reverence continues today. Cultures as disparate as the Ainu in northern Japan, the tribes of the Pacific Northwest and commercial fishermen along Alaska's coast cling to their "first fish" celebrations, welcoming the salmon home again every spring. Urban residents are cleaning up long-abandoned salmon streams in hopes of seeing the miracle of the spawn once again. There is even talk of dynamiting dams in the Pacific

FACING PAGE: *The purse seiner* Talia *fishes for pink salmon in Chatham Strait. (Ed LeDoux)*

Northwest, solely so salmon can reclaim the waters that once were theirs.

Such efforts may seem impractical in a world where hunting has largely given way to cultivation. Chalk it up to the power of salmon, but to many it seems only right given that *Homo sapiens* is the newcomer to the planet. The first salmon, *Eosalmo driftwoodensis*, swam prehistoric seas 50 million years ago. By the time fire-using, spear-throwing humans traipsed down the shoreline of North America the modern salmon was more than 1 million years old.

By virtue of its abundance and annual recurrence, the genus *Oncorhynchus* ("hook-nosed") helped shape civilizations around the North Pacific. Salmon were easily obtained in a few weeks of summer work. High in protein and fat, the nutritional value was not lost in preservation. Dried or smoked, salmon were easy to transport and to save for the winter, and plentiful enough to feed dog teams, which in turn provided winter transportation. Anthropologists believe that salmon gave aboriginal North Americans leisure time that few cultures enjoyed, which they used to develop a rich and artistic lifestyle, particularly in Southeast Alaska and British Columbia.

The Russian fur trader and entrepreneur Gregorii Shelikhov is credited with the first commercial salmon fishing business in Alaska. He started a drying operation on the west side of Kodiak Island in 1785 to feed his *promyshlenniki*, the Cossack raiders he brought along as fur hunters and managers. By the turn of the 18th century, the Northwest Co. was selling wooden casks of salted salmon at many of its outposts along the coast.

The roots of Alaska's salmon industry were just as firmly planted in California, however, when Hopgood, Hume Co. started canning salmon on the Sacramento River in 1864. The methods were crude — each can was cut from sheet tin, rolled by hand

and fitted with lids, then soldered shut before it could be run through the retort for sterilization. But the product proved immensely popular and within a few years the technology had spread northward to take advantage of the great fisheries on the Columbia River and in Alaska.

OF TRAPS AND PIRATES

American salmon processors pounced on Alaska shortly after the United States bought the territory from Russia in 1867, opening several salteries in Southeast. The first two canneries began operating in 1878. Within a decade processing plants dotted the new territory from Ketchikan to Kodiak and Bristol Bay. By the Great Depression more than 150 plants around Alaska came alive every summer with the sounds of canning machinery — the sounds of money being made.

It was a foreign sound in much of Alaska. For millennia, the Native fishermen had had the fish to them-selves, catching what they needed and no more. When commercial fishing

Skip Hermansen, Roy Shapley, Paul Stevens and his grandson Johnny launch a skiff during a Cook Inlet sockeye setnet fishery. The fishermen put the skiff into the surf and nose it into a swell. Skip, in the bow, pulls on a line to help move the skiff into deeper water. (Ed LeDoux)

began in earnest, the canneries hired some Natives, but imported the majority of their workers from San Francisco and Seattle. The new fishermen had cannery-supplied boats and modern nets, and virtually no limits on how, when or where they could fish. The canneries' demand for fish was the only limit on the catch.

Among the "fishing practices" in the new territory was barricading entire streams and dipping out the salmon that collected. In 1889

Congress banned the barricades but didn't fund any enforcement effort until 1892, when two agents were hired but given no transportation money. They relied on cannery vessels to get around the territory.

Only slightly less onerous was the fish trap, which appeared in Alaska waters in 1885 and soon was ubiquitous. The traps were expensive to build, but deadly efficient — so efficient they eventually were banned in California, Oregon, Washington

and British Columbia. Early efforts to remove them in Alaska failed, in part because the canneries themselves owned upwards of 90 percent of the traps and the cannery owners exercised greater political power than those who would outlaw them.

Traps relied on a fencelike lead — some as long as 3 miles — built perpendicular to the beach that directed the fish into a corral, or pot, from which they could not escape. Unlike fishermen, traps operated non-stop, night and day. The fish were held in the pot until the cannery needed them. Occasionally the pots were opened and fish allowed to escape, but frequently the salmon remained trapped until they were used or beyond use. One federal observer reported from Bristol Bay in 1900 "winrows (sic) of decaying fish, a hundred feet in width, along the beach, testify to the enormous waste during a canning season."

Almost from the beginning, a schism appeared between Alaska residents and the industry they called the "Fish Trust" — the Seattle- and San Francisco-based companies that owned the majority of traps, boats and plants, and the federal bureaucrats who managed them. Most Alaskans viewed commercial fishing as a means of settling the state. Fishing and fish packing could provide summer employment and money for a family to make it through the winters — but only if the fisheries were managed to last. Judging by the rapidly depleted salmon stocks to the south, Alaskans guessed their fisheries would be next unless they gained some control.

But their attempts to rein in the Fish Trust were stymied by the

For the first time the Wood River near Dillingham was opened to a sockeye salmon driftnet fishery in 1996. Impetus for the opening was to conserve coho salmon stocks in the nearby Nushagak River. By opening the Wood River, ADF&G commercial fish biologists were able to ease fishing pressure on the coho salmon in the Nushagak. The 1996 commercial sockeye take out of the Wood River was about 70,000 fish. The Wood River was again open to sockeye driftnet commercial fishing beginning in July 1997, this time with a goal of addressing an imbalance in the sockeye escapements for the Wood and Nushagak rivers. In 1997 there were far more sockeye in the Wood River than in the Nushagak. Fishing was ongoing as of mid-July, but commercial fish biologists think they have at least reached minimum sockeye escapement for the Nushagak. (Greg Syverson)

Linnea Kistler LeBeau, Bob Woods (left) and Kevin Culpon collect sockeye salmon from a setnet sight in Tuxedni Bay. Linnea is the granddaughter of Joe Fribrock, founder of the abandoned Snug Harbor Cannery on Chisik Island. Fribrock began the cannery in the 1920s when fishermen fished upper Cook Inlet in wooden boats sometimes referred to as "snug boats." (Sundog Photography)

canneries' lobbying efforts in Washington, D.C. Proposed legislation was routinely given to the processors for their comments, and routinely adjusted to meet their approval, as when a major conservation effort was attempted in 1894. It sought to close every fishing area of Alaska once a week to allow salmon to swim upstream to spawn; the processors' lobby got Bristol Bay, Cook Inlet and Prince William Sound excluded. Research was non-existent and enforcement was negligible. One agent in 1908 visited 34 fish traps and found 29 "brazenly violating" the few laws extant. He returned in two weeks to find 24 still in violation.

Eventually Alaskans took matters into their own hands. Some robbed the traps at gunpoint. Others formed fishermen's unions to exert economic pressure wherever possible. Finally they united in the drive for statehood that culminated in 1959. One of the first actions of the new Alaska State Legislature was to ban fish traps forever.

FACING PAGE: *Fishing boats line a dock at St. Herman's Harbor at Kodiak, headquarters for much of the Gulf of Alaska fishing fleet. (Harry M. Walker)*

ABOVE: *A fishermen mends his net. The state of Alaska regulates the mesh size, the measurement from knot to knot after the net is taut, of a net and the size varies with the different fish species. (Harry M. Walker)*

RIGHT: *Fishing nets are spread for repair at Kodiak. (Harry M. Walker)*

The F/V Sunset *picks up ice from Excursion Inlet Packing for an early season Chatham Strait troll opening in May 1996. Trolling boats in Southeast are among the most beautiful boats in Alaska. (Christian Racich)*

NEW WAY

To ensure a clear break from territorial days, the authors of the Alaska Constitution wrote a separate article on natural resources. The only one of its kind in the United States, it mandates that Alaska's fish and game shall be made available to the people, but managed on "the basis of sustained yield" — that is, to last forever.

That didn't look likely in the years shortly after statehood. Many salmon stocks were in deplorable condition and by the early 1970s had hit their lowest levels since the turn of the century. State biologists severely restricted commercial catches to ensure adequate spawning escapement; some areas never even opened during those bleak years.

The dire situation made it easy for Alaska voters to pass, in 1970, a radical proposal never before tried in the United States called "limited entry." It limited the number of fishermen in each area and gave them exclusive rights to harvest the fish.

Limited entry eliminated the "tragedy of the commons," in which no one protects the property that belongs to all. Now each fishery has a small constituency of permit holders who fight to ensure it is properly managed and protected from plundering.

As with any commodity, however, limited entry permits now are bought and sold on the open market, with the price determined by supply and demand. Salmon permits for areas that promise a good return have cost nearly $400,000; others can be had for $10,000 or less, though the yield is equally meager.

The restrictions of the 1970s soon paid off. Salmon stocks began to increase, aided by superb environmental conditions as well as constraints on Japanese salmon fisheries conducted on the high seas. In Alaska's first century of commercial fishing, 1878-1978, the annual harvest topped 100 million salmon just six times. From 1980 to 1996, the catch hit that milestone every year but one, and in 1995 reached the 200 million mark for the first time.

Alaska's superb runs during the last two decades stand in stark contrast to those of the Pacific Northwest, which were decimated not by commercial fishing so much as habitat loss. The

mighty Columbia River, which once boasted runs totaling 16 million fish, has been choked by more than a dozen hydroelectric dams. Logging in both the United States and Canada has fouled streams where salmon once spawned. Diversion canals that allow alfalfa to bloom in former deserts occasionally deposit full-grown salmon in the fields. Several fish stocks are on the endangered species list.

Alaskans have tried to learn from the mistakes of the Pacific Northwest and to date their efforts have paid off.

At some time, however, environmental conditions could change, natural production may decline, and the seasons of 100-million harvests will seem like the good old days.

Biologists and fishermen around the world marvel at Alaska's salmon conservation success. At the helm of this juggernaut is the Alaska Board of Fisheries, a seven-member panel of Alaska residents — some with commercial fishing background, some without, all of them volunteers — who meet 40 to 50 days a year to chart the progress

Fishermen are notoriously inventive, but the creator of this vessel in Bristol Bay is legendary. His "Moby Duck" is a former military landing craft outfitted to drift gillnet, then drive ashore to deliver the catch. (Art Sutch)

SALMON ECONOMICS

Alaska salmon not long ago were the dominant force in world markets, providing nearly half the product that filled freezers and shelf space from Tokyo to Topeka. When Alaska had a big catch, prices dropped worldwide, and when the harvest was skimpy, the value of all salmon rose.

In the late 1970s, however, the salmon business changed. Not only did Alaska's natural runs start a meteoric rise that had not stopped as of 1996, but a new competitor emerged on the scene, farmed salmon.

Unlike the salmon ranching done in Alaska, in which juvenile fish are released into the ocean and then harvested alongside wild salmon when they return a year or more later, salmon farmers raise the fish in floating net pens from juvenile to adult. With harvest time set by the market, not Mother Nature, fresh salmon are now available in seafood shops and restaurants year-round.

The response to farmed fish has been nothing short of phenomenal. In 1980, just 15 million pounds were sold world-wide. In a decade sales had hit 620 million pounds, and are anticipated to top 1 billion pounds by the year 2000.

The biggest producers are Norway and Chile, but Scotland, Ireland, Canada and even Maine and Washington have salmon farms. After intense debate, the Alaska Legislature upheld the state's prohibition against salmon mariculture in the late 1980s, though the law does allow shellfish farming.

Just as salmon production has turned topsy-turvy in the last two decades, so have salmon prices. Buoyed by a string of average production years in Alaska and an economic boom in Japan that saw consumers' buying power triple, salmon prices hit record levels in 1988. Fish buyers bid up the price of Bristol Bay sockeyes to $2.25 a pound, and every other fish price followed suit. Statewide, salmon netted almost $800 million.

But in the ensuing years Japan's economy fizzled, Alaska fishermen set a string of new harvest records and farmed fish production shot up. A sockeye worth $20 in 1988 fetched just $5 in 1994, and pink salmon worth 75 cents a pound in 1988 brought only 10 cents a pound by 1996.

Price fluctuations have always been part of the fishing life, but no one had ever seen price declines like that. Some fishermen mothballed their boats and nets, others bought permits in areas where the volume was higher, and some invested in their operations — adding a $20,000 refrigeration system in Bristol Bay boosted the sockeye price by several cents a pound for their fish. Permit prices have declined, but

Pinks are the most numerous, yet lowest value, of Alaska's five salmon species. (Joel Gay)

fuel, food and insurance costs continue to climb.

Industry observers agree that the only way out of the price abyss is to boost demand for salmon — particularly Alaska salmon. The emerging markets of Asia are often touted as the hope of the future, though the United States is also ripe for improved salmon sales. The average American eats less than half a pound of salmon per year, but nearly 4 pounds of tuna. Marketing efforts increased substantially after a statewide salmon tax devoted to marketing won approval in 1991. Support for the levy waned, however, as prices remained low.

Fishermen have improved the overall quality of their catch over the years by adding refrigeration systems and adopting better handling techniques. Processors continue to look for new preparation methods to make it easier for consumers to prepare salmon at home, such as flavored salmon fillets in microwaveable pouches.

Still, a substantial portion of Alaska's harvest every year is either canned or frozen whole and shipped to Japan, and until these major market sectors show a willingness to pay more when other options such as farmed salmon, tuna and cheap chicken and beef are available, prices are not likely to return to 1988 levels any time soon. ◄

Trollers ride a swell off Yakobi Rock on the west side of Yakobi Island in Southeast. (Don Cornelius)

entire fishing region on a moment's notice to ensure enough fish get upstream to spawn or that the excess can be harvested by fishermen.

It's an enormous job, said Bob Clasby, director of ADF&G's Commercial Fisheries Management and Development Division. "Not only is there the biological management," he said, "but the direction of benefits — carrying out the board's allocation and trying to figure out who gets what fish. It takes a lot of time, people and money. But I think the return on the investment the state puts into it is pretty good."

CHINOOK SALMON

On a cold winter morning in January with the sun little more than a cool gold disk in a pale blue sky, the first Alaska salmon fishery of the year is well under way. The skipper stands alone in the stern, driving slowly along the rugged coast. Fishing alone this time of year, there is no crew chatter, no sound but the heavy thrum of the diesel engine and the occasional tinkle of a bell hung from one of the long poles that extend over the water, making the boat look like a mechanical daddy longlegs.

When the "tattletale" rings, the

and future of the state's fisheries. Appointed by the governor, confirmed by the Legislature and advised by a statewide network of local committees, the board sets the policies that are, in turn, enacted by the Alaska Department of Fish and Game (ADF&G).

With nearly 800 full- and part-time biologists, biometricians, statisticians and secretaries in almost two dozen offices, ADF&G manages the commercial fisheries for salmon, herring, crab and several dozen other species. The cost in 1996 was about $43 million, which enabled Alaska fisher-

men to earn some $1.2 billion. In turn, fishermen contributed almost $69 million to the state treasury in fees and taxes.

Although many of the state fisheries date back 100 years or more, they are constantly monitored and frequently adjusted. In territorial days, regulations were often decided months ahead of time and quick decisions were impossible because they first had to be published in the Federal Register — a 72-hour process at best. Salmon often suffered as a result. Now biologists can open and close a single stream or an fisherman reels in one of the stainless steel lines trailing the boat. Soon he sees the flash of silver that quickens the heart and brings a smile to a fisherman's face. Holding the leader in one hand and a long-handled hook in the other, he deftly gaffs the fish, and in one smooth motion swings a 25-pound, rainbow-hued chinook salmon out of the water and onto the deck.

The skipper returns the lucky lure to the sea, hoping it will catch another. With a few slices of a razor-sharp knife, he quickly cleans the fish. When it's washed and glistening again he packs its belly full of ice and sets it carefully alongside others lying in the hold as if it were a package of dollar bills in a bank vault. In a night or two, this fish could be dinner in a white-tablecloth restaurant in San Francisco or New York, and trollers handle each fish with utmost respect.

Of the five species of salmon found in Alaska, chinook, or king salmon, are the best known. Perhaps it's their size — chinooks frequently exceed 50 pounds and the record is 123 — and perhaps it's the white-glove treatment that king salmon receive when caught, but there is something magical about Alaska's state fish, *Oncorhynchus tshawytscha*. Even the small ones have a majesty and vitality that make

most other salmon seem anemic by comparison.

Chinooks are caught throughout Alaska, but are most plentiful in Southeast. Like several other salmon species, chinooks have large black spots on the back and tail, but if the gums are black, not gray, it's a king.

Not every salmon will eagerly strike a lure, which makes the chinook a favored quarry of troll fishermen. A troller — not to be confused with a trawler — is easily identifiable in a harbor: Look for boats with two or three long, skinny poles standing

upright on each side of the cabin. When fishing, the trolling poles are lowered to almost horizontal. Two to six stainless steel lines trail off the poles, each weighted with a heavy lead "cannonball." Also attached to each steel line are a dozen or more heavy nylon leaders with a lure or baited hook. Most trollers use hydraulic power to retrieve their lines. Some still use hand-powered reels, or gurdies, however, and are known as hand trollers.

Many consider trollers to be the artisans of the commercial salmon fisheries. They not only must know

Grant Trask lands a king salmon off Biorka Island west of Sitka. (Don Cornelius)

where to fish, but which lures to use and how to get the fish aboard without losing them. Two trollers working side by side can have markedly different catches, simply because one skipper chose red hoochies while the other used green or gold.

Southeast is the only region of Alaska where trolling is still allowed. As late as 1976 trollers could fish in coastal waters all year from Southeast to Kodiak. As salmon stocks declined in Alaska and elsewhere along the Pacific coast, however, the trollers' grounds were reduced in the name of conservation. Even though Alaska stocks have rebounded, the troll fleet still cannot leave Southeast. In fact, their chinook season has been reduced to just a few days every summer and several months in the winter, beginning in October. Out of necessity, they began to fish for other salmon species and now coho salmon constitute the majority of their harvest.

The trollers' problem is inherent in all salmon fisheries: interceptions. It was not known until about 1940, but salmon are migratory, spending one or more years circling the open ocean after leaving their natal stream. Chinooks, which live in freshwater for up to three years before they swim to the sea, circumnavigate the North Pacific for up to four years, swimming thousands of miles and feeding on zooplankton, squid and small fish.

By tagging juvenile salmon and tracing the tags when the fish were caught as adults, biologists learned that salmon are often caught far from their natal streams. Complaints by fishermen in Kodiak and Prince William Sound spurred the first reductions in trollers' fishing grounds.

An even bigger restraint on the Southeast troll fleet came in 1985 with the Pacific Salmon Treaty. Signed after some 20 years of negotiations between the United States and Canada, it governs "trans-national fish" — those that spawn in Canada but are caught by U.S. fishermen, or vice versa. The Southeast Panhandle and British

Kathleen Wendt counts tagged chum salmon at a weir on Fish Creek near Hyder in Southeast. Biologists cut the adipose fin of salmon that were implanted with a tagging devise when they were young. Kathleen watches for these fish to return, nets and kills them, cuts off their head and sends the head to ADF&G biologists. (Lance Peck)

Columbia are riddled with such runs, but the treaty also covers the Yukon River far to the north and the Columbia River to the south.

Though five species of salmon and numerous fisheries are affected by the salmon treaty, trollers have been the hardest hit. The pact limited Southeast Alaska's chinook harvest to fewer than 300,000 a year — far below the trollers' pre-treaty average. Though stocks have increased in the meantime, the treaty will keep the lid on Alaska catches at least through

Seiners fish for pink salmon near Valdez in Prince William Sound. (James L. Davis)

2000, forcing trollers to go out in midwinter in hopes of hearing the "tattletale" ring.

LEFT: *Skip Hermansen hefts a king salmon taken while picking a setnet for sockeyes. The fishermen get mostly sockeyes because kings usually break through the net. (Ed LeDoux)*

ABOVE: *Sometimes fishermen don't like the prices they are being offered for their fish and they strike. (Joel Gay)*

FACING PAGE: *A fisherman rides in the crow's nest and another stands nearby, both searching for pink salmon in Tutka Bay off Kachemak Bay in lower Cook Inlet. The crew in the skiff await a signal from the spotters to begin playing out the net. (Sundog Photography)*

PINK SALMON

On a hot summer day in a shallow lagoon in Prince William Sound, a gleaming white fishing boat prowls the green-black water like a sleek jungle cat. The skipper stands in the crow's nest high above, peering intently at big, dark areas in the water that appear to the casual observer to be rocks. But these rocks slowly move.

Two crew members stand on deck, alert, silent and safely behind a haystack of net. Snubbed tight to the seiner's stern is a powerful aluminum skiff, its engine running and the skiff operator watching the skipper as intently as the skipper eyes the black ball of fish.

Then comes the cry, "Let 'er go!" and the tranquil lagoon quickly fills with blue smoke, white water and noise. The skiff leaps away from the big boat, towing the net's end in a wide circle. Simultaneously the skipper "firewalls" the seiner and completes the arc toward the oncoming skiff. When they meet, they have drawn a curtain of net around a school of pink salmon, catching thousands of fish in a single swipe. It's the most efficient way to catch salmon legally in Alaska, particularly for the most ubiquitous of the species, the pink.

Also known as "humpies" for the prominent humpback the males develop prior to spawning, pinks are the smallest of Alaska's salmon and, by virtue of their low oil content and pale flesh, the least valuable per pound.

But what *Oncorhynchus gorbuscha* lacks in individual value it makes up in volume. Pinks are the most abundant of Alaska's salmon catch — up to 128 million fish in a single season, compared with an average chinook harvest of less than 600,000. Most pink salmon are canned, though increasingly processors are seeking other forms of packaging, including freezing them in filet form or grinding the meat and forming it into nuggets, hams and sausage.

Pink salmon are readily identified by their tiny, fine-grained scales. Like chinooks, they too have big black spots on the back and tail, but the fine scales are a giveaway every time. The fastest growing of Alaska's salmon, pink fry swim to the ocean the spring after they are spawned, and a year later they're back, weighing 3 to 4 pounds.

For their quick growth, pinks were the species of choice to raise in

The skiff helps move a purse seiner once the net has been brought on board. (Christian Racich)

When a purse seiner catches a big school of salmon, the fish are often dipped out one scoop at a time with a brailer. (Joel Gay)

hatcheries. In the 1970s, fishermen throughout Alaska decided to try their luck at fish ranching — releasing fry into the ocean in hopes that enough would come back the following summer to make a substantial catch. Up to one-third of the returning fish could be harvested by the hatchery to pay for its operations, with the remainder available to the fleet.

ADF&G built more than a dozen hatcheries, though budget cuts eventually forced the state to relinquish their operations to non-profit, fishermen-funded aquaculture associations. Hatcheries are now found all over Alaska except Bristol Bay, and all five salmon species are raised.

During the mid-1980s, when salmon prices were high, the hatcheries were a boon. In some areas, hatchery-raised fish comprised as much as three-fourths of the total harvest. Statewide, enhancement programs contribute about 15 percent of the catch.

But the record runs in recent years, boosted in part by hatcheries, have added to a glut of fish on world markets and salmon prices have fallen by about 50 percent during the 1990s. With lower prices it takes more fish to pay for the hatcheries, leaving fewer for fishermen to harvest. That, in

turn, calls into question the cost-effectiveness of the programs. Many fishermen and processors believe the industry should emphasize quality, not quantity, and some hatcheries have been shut down until prices rise again.

Seiners target not only pink salmon, but any species that runs in great number. Though several kinds of seines have been developed around the world, Alaska fishermen use purse seines. The boats are recognizable by the haystack of net webbing and corks piled on the stern.

A seiner that circles a school of fish

quickly is said to make a "round haul." When the fish are traveling up the coast, a skipper will lay the net out perpendicular to the beach, with the skiff holding the net tightly to the shore. The seiner then pulls its end into the current, creating a hook-shape. After "holding a hook" for half an hour or so, the seiner and skiff close up the net by driving toward each, again making a circle. Once they meet, the net is hauled in in the same fashion as in a round haul.

The state limits the length, depth and even the mesh size of seines as a

The skiff operator is a key player in a smooth-running purse seine operation. This skiffman awaits instructions from the skipper while fishing in Amalga Harbor northwest of Juneau. (Christian Racich)

means of limiting a boat's efficiency. But seines, like all other types of salmon gear, catch whatever happens to swim by, and seiners all over Alaska have had their fishing time and areas restricted to reduce the incidental catch of salmon bound for distant streams.

SOCKEYE SALMON

Even from a distance the North Line looks mean. Perhaps Alaska's most infamous fishing area, it is no more than a line on the charts of Bristol Bay defining the northern boundary of the Egegik District. Like many lines, however, this one has a power all its own.

A black pall hangs over it and boats swarm like angry ants, their antennae prickly on the horizon. On the line itself are crowded hundreds of boats the size of city buses, and each is in constant, chaotic motion. Some run at full speed with nets flying over their stern rollers and exhaust belching from their stacks. Others drive aimlessly, each threading a different course through the crowd. Boats occasionally bang into one another with a sickening crunch.

The crews are quiet on deck, but colorful sign language issues from every flying bridge. Skippers fling their arms to the heavens, hunch their shoulders, shake their heads and jab their fingers into the air as if pointing could move a 32-foot boat.

And they shout, constantly, at each other and their crews, for simple communication or to relieve their frustration. They yell until they're hoarse, or the offender leaves, or the fishing period is over, or they simply can't take it any more. They may drive away from the madness, but they always come back to the North Line because it's the surest place in Bristol Bay to find fish.

Of all the fisheries in Alaska, surely the craziest is Bristol Bay. Just four weeks long, it is the shortest salmon fishery in the state, yet the richest because of its target: sockeyes.

If kings are the aristocracy and pinks the common masses of the salmon world, sockeyes, or red salmon, are the upper middle class. They are the money fish, generally commanding the highest prices from buyers and consequently the most interest from fishermen. Prized by Japanese consumers for their firm, red flesh and high oil content, sockeyes set the base price from which all other salmon prices are derived. Originally favored for canning, now some 85 percent of the sockeye pack is frozen and sold in Japan.

After coming out of the stream bed gravel, *Oncorhynchus nerka* spends at least one summer and one winter in a lake, feeding on zooplankton and preparing for its journey out to sea. It swims to saltwater in its second or third spring and spends another two to three years migrating and fattening before returning to spawn. Adults typically weigh 4 to 8 pounds; the statewide average is about 6 pounds.

Fresh out of the water, sockeyes have olive-green topsides that quickly turn indigo, hence the moniker "blueback." Sockeyes have only fine speckling and are easily confused with chums. The best way to distinguish between the two is by hand — bend open the gill cover and peek inside. A sockeye has 28 to 40 gill rakers (bars of toothlike material that protect the sensitive gill material and act as food filters for salmon and other fishes), where a chum has 19 to 26. In addition, sockeye gill rakers are long, slender and rough or even serrated; chums' are short, stout and smooth.

Gillnets catch most of Alaska's sockeyes. Unlike a seine, a gillnet

As the crew hauls in a seiner's net, it is carefully stacked to ensure that it goes out correctly during the next set. (Christian Racich)

catches fish individually. The net is a flat band of webbing 12 to more than 20 feet deep suspended between the corkline and leadline. Rather than encircle a school, it entangles the fish that swim into it — usually by the gills, but sometimes by the tail, jaw or even a single fin. Gillnet fishermen develop strong hands and aching wrists from a summer of wrestling fish out of the net.

Because salmon avoid a net they can see, gillnets work best in murky water. The mesh size of the net — measured from knot to knot after stretching the web tight — varies depending on the target species, but for sockeyes is around 5 inches. As with seines, the state regulates the length, depth and mesh size of gillnets.

If the net is towed behind a boat, it is a drift gillnet. If anchored to the beach it is considered a set gillnet, or setnet. Most drift boats are readily identified by the 4-foot-high reel, mounted in either the stern or bow, on which the net is wound, though a few fishermen in western Alaska still haul their nets by hand. When the skipper

LIMITED ENTRY

Once a salmon tender has full holds, it, too, must deliver its load. This one is offloading its high-value sockeye catch at a shore plant in Bristol Bay. (Chlaus Lotscher)

Alaska's limited entry program created 11,700 salmon permits, 77 percent of which are held by Alaska residents. Many of today's fishermen were the original recipients, but those who were not can buy into any fishery they can afford. Some are easier to afford than others, and none is a get-rich-quick scheme.

For example, the average price of an Area M drift gillnet permit in 1995 was $305,000, according to the Alaska Commercial Fisheries Entry Commission, and the average permit holder grossed $135,000. Not bad, you might say — unless you bought a permit in 1993 when they cost nearly $400,000.

And though many would love to earn $135,000 in four months, the numbers are deceptive. Skipper Mike Nakada, who fished there at the time but has since quit, said he paid one-third of his earnings to the crew. Off his share came $20,000 a year in boat payments plus $20,000 for the permit itself. Food, fuel and insurance trimmed $20,000 more, he said, and while buying a full set of new nets could cost $20,000, Nakada repaired or replaced them as needed — at roughly $5,000 a year in materials plus two to three weeks of work for him and his two-man crew in May. Fishing began in early June and ended around mid-September, and he fished every day in between — about 100 days straight except for a 10-day stretch in mid-July that he called his "sanity break."

Perhaps trolling sounds better. Old, wooden troll boats are relatively cheap — $10,000 for one that probably will make it through a season or two. A hand troll permit in 1995 was available for just $7,400. A person can fish alone for much of the season, buying only fuel, insurance, groceries and enough jigs and hoochies to entice the cohos to bite. But expect to make meager pay. In 1995, hand trollers grossed just $3,200 for their summer and winter of work. ◄

Purse seine crew members often wear their rain gear while retrieving the net to keep the water, seaweed, jellyfish and other marine life that is wrung out of the net also out of their hair. (Danny Daniels)

is ready to start fishing, a crew member throws the end of the net overboard attached to a large buoy. Once the net is played out, the skipper can either drift or tow the net until it's time to reel it in and pick the fish. One drift might last a few minutes or a few hours, depending on how many fish are hitting the net.

A drift boat's mobility creates freedom, but also intense competition, especially at the border of a fishing district. Wherever salmon enter a district, skippers jockey to be first in line. Whoever is "first net" when the reds are running strong at the North Line of Bristol Bay's Egegik District or north of there at the Johnson-Hill Line in the Naknek-Kvichak District can expect to catch so many salmon that the net may actually sink after just a few minutes of fishing.

Few fishermen sink their nets, however. Because salmon swim the same direction as the current, the boat that sets its net on the district boundary quickly drifts back into the district. Another boat then sets in front of the first, then another, and soon the first boat is catching nothing. In the parlance of fishermen, he was

"corked." Then it's time to haul in the net, pick the fish, and jostle for position on the line and the chance to cork someone else.

If agents of the Alaska Division of Fish and Wildlife Protection — essentially sea-going State Troopers — are there to police the district boundaries, fishermen are usually beyond reproach. But as soon as enforcement agents leave, some skippers will edge over the line. Law-abiding fishermen find it frustrating, but there is little that can be done as the state trims back its budget, including that of the fish cops.

Setnets work like driftnets, except

the net is anchored perpendicular to the beach. Most setnetters work out of small skiffs and pick their nets as the fish accumulate. Others wait until the tide goes out and collect their fish while standing on dry ground.

Before reds reach the shores of Bristol Bay, however, they must run a gauntlet known as "False Pass," actually a series of passes at the tip of Alaska Peninsula between the North Pacific and Bristol Bay. Its official name is Area M, which includes both the south and north sides of the Alaska Peninsula, plus the Aleutian Islands, but it could easily be called Grand Central Station West. For more than

A troll fishermen hooks a coho or silver salmon in Southeast. (Don Cornelius)

100 years fishermen have worked the area with success; tagging studies show that they catch salmon from Japan, Russia, northwest Alaska, Kodiak, even Prince William Sound.

But in June, the vast majority are Bristol Bay-bound sockeye. The Area M interception was one of the first issues taken up by the Board of Fisheries after statehood. Fishing times and areas have been adjusted time and again, but not until 1975 was the sockeye catch capped. Since then Bristol Bay fishermen have given up 8.3 percent of their catch every year to "False Pass," and like the volcanoes that form the spine of the Alaska Peninsula, some are still fuming.

CHUM SALMON

Where the Bering Sea and North Pacific rub shoulders, it seems to rain incessantly, and on a June night not far from False Pass the rain has a cold, mean feel. It doesn't fall so much as slice through the air, though it doesn't faze the skipper of an Area M seiner tied alongside a tender to deliver. He complains of the meager catch — 20,000 pounds of salmon in the last 12 hours. "I've had days when we got 90,000 pounds, when we were full by 2 o'clock," he says angrily. "There's no future in this."

His boat is a finely tuned, $1.5 million fish-catching machine that he keeps busy most of the year chasing herring, cod, crab and halibut. It's 58 feet long, nearly 30 feet wide, and can carry 100,000 pounds in the refrigerated holds. He has filled it many times, but tonight it seems too big.

Nearly 400 miles to the north, another skipper makes a delivery on another wet June night. A Yukon River gillnetter, his boat is 24 feet long — small enough that three could fit side-by-side on the seiner's deck like aluminum sardines. He, too, is miffed about the catch — 1,500 pounds. He's had days when he landed 6,000. "There's no future in this," he grouses.

The two fishermen are linked by chum salmon, which pass through Area M on their way to the Arctic-Yukon-Kuskokwim Region. The fish are also called "dog" salmon because they were the primary winter fuel for the sled dog teams used throughout the Arctic. In recent years, however, AYK fishermen have relied on chums for much of their annual income. Meager as it is — a fraction of what most fishermen earn elsewhere in Alaska — commercial fishing is critical, buying fuel for snow machines, ammunition for rifles and other goods necessary to live off the land as their forebears have for millennia.

Like pink salmon, *Oncorhynchus keta* swim downriver the spring after hatching. Instead of returning after a single year at sea, however, chums cruise the North Pacific for two to five years and grow as large as 30 pounds, though typical commercial catches are 8 to 10 pounds. Strong swimmers, they sometimes surge against a net so hard they pull the corks underwater.

Fresh out of saltwater, chums appear similar to sockeyes: greenish-blue with only fine speckling and no large spots. Many fishermen claim to distinguish the two species by the size of their golden irises — chums' are larger. Biologists rely on gill raker size and number. Chums have fewer but stouter gill rakers, while the sockeye's are greater in both number and length. Once chums reach freshwater, however, their true colors show. Distinctive vertical bars of green or purple appear on their sides and the males develop a hooked snout and enormous, doglike teeth. In that state they are known variously as "calicoes" and "alligators."

Chums are the world travelers of the salmon species, found in wider distribution than any other — from central California to the Arctic Ocean, from coastal Japan and Russia to the headwaters of the Yukon River some 2,300 miles from saltwater. They are targeted by seiners and gillnetters all over Alaska but are the primary species for many Interior Alaska fishermen. Unlike the rest of Alaska, much of the commercial fishing effort in northwest Alaska is in fresh water. Most of the fishing is done with gillnets, both drift and set.

In the upper Yukon drainage, however, chums are caught in a unique operation, the fishwheel. Powered by the river's current, the fishwheel methodically dips its baskets into the water, scoops up salmon like a Ferris wheel picking up passengers, then deposits them into a collection box. Some fishermen use wire or nylon mesh leads to direct the salmon into their fishwheel's path, and can adjust the wheel closer or farther from the bank and up and down in the water to increase their harvest. Only about 170 fishwheels are permitted for commercial use.

Another fishery that uses fish wheels is known as subsistence — fishing for personal use or barter. The catch cannot be sold, which sets it apart from commercial fishing. Chums are the primary subsistence fish in northwest

Most salmon setnetters fish out of skiffs, bringing the net over the side rail rather than the bow or stern. This pair fish for chum salmon in the northernmost commercial salmon fishery in Alaska, in Kotzebue Sound. A couple decades ago this was a profitable fishery that allowed families to earn their income for a year with a few weeks of fishing. In recent years, the fish runs have declined and many fishermen have left the fishery. (Seth Kantner)

FACING PAGE: *Kuskokwim River salmon fishermen line up to unload their catch at Bethel. (Don Pitcher)*

ABOVE: *One of the many headaches faced by commercial fishermen is catching a net in a propeller, a situation that sometimes can be worked out by hand, as this crew is trying to do, and sometimes requires rescue, even to the extent of bringing in a diver. (Joel Gay)*

RIGHT: *The purse seiner F/V* Archangel *fishes near Sitka. (Christian Racich)*

Alaska; chinooks, sockeyes and cohos are popular elsewhere in the state. Many Alaskans, both urban and rural, participate in subsistence fishing, which requires only Alaska residency and a free permit. The fisheries have their own regulations, gear restrictions and seasons, and are managed by ADF&G.

While subsistence fishing accounts for less than 1 percent of the salmon harvested statewide, the fisheries have become extremely significant to commercial fishermen. The Alaska Constitution says the state's fish and game are equally available to all residents. But in times of shortage, the Alaska Supreme Court has ruled, subsistence fisheries will be the last curtailed. Commercial and sport fishing must always be limited first.

Such scarcity has rarely been a problem. In 1993, however, biologists closed commercial, sport and finally subsistence fisheries throughout the AYK Region for conservation reasons. Local residents were furious, and demanded that the Board of Fisheries reduce the chum catch in Area M. When the board refused, they sued.

The board agreed with ADF&G biologists that there was no proven biological link between the Area M fishery and the AYK shortages. The Commissioner of Fish and Game then stepped in and unilaterally reduced the chum catch, which brought a countersuit by Area M fishermen. A judge told the governor to settle the matter; the governor upheld his commissioner's decision. The Alaska Supreme Court overruled them both, saying allocation should be left to the Board of Fisheries.

The furor over chums is not unique to Area M. Their low cost has made chum salmon increasingly popular in U.S. markets in recent years, but their eggs are often worth more than the fish themselves. Salmon roe is a delicacy in Japan, Russia and Europe, and chum roe is considered the best for its size, color and flavor. Although it is illegal in Alaska to dump fish carcasses after extracting only the roe, non-profit hatcheries received special dispensation in 1996 to "roe-strip" chums they had raised in record numbers.

Fishermen and processors cried foul, saying that if they couldn't roe-strip, the hatcheries shouldn't either. After the season, all parties agreed that every effort should be made to use the chum carcasses however possible, including shipping them to food banks for free distribution, and the roe-stripping provision was lifted.

COHO SALMON

Yellow cottonwood leaves flutter along the shore and the sun is low in the sky when a troller hears the "tattletale" ring. "That's it, last fish," he tells himself, and begins reeling in. The season has been long and fraught with concern — over price, closures for other species, a foreign sound he doesn't like whenever he starts the diesel. Now it's time for fall projects,

The gillnetter Kenaitze *cruises on the Kenai River while other boats wait at a processing facility at Kenai. (Sundog Photography)*

getting the kids ready for school, perhaps even a bit of fly-fishing for steelhead on that stream near Yakutat.

He enjoys the salmon's surge, the way it rolls in the dark water almost angrily, as he prepares to swing the gaff one final time. When it clears the water he can tell by its size it's not a chinook, and when he cleans the fish he keeps the eggs for himself. After a final rinse, he lays the fish in an empty cooler. Sautéed with butter, garlic and lemon pepper, it will make a delicious dinner for his family.

Big, bright and feisty, coho salmon, also known as silvers, are usually the last of the salmon runs every year. One of the three spotted salmon, *Oncorhynchus kisutch* is distinguished by the blush of silver that graces its tail. Bigger than pinks — cohos typically weigh 8 to 12 pounds — they can be confused with small chinooks. But their tails have spots only on the upper half, and their gums are gray, not black.

When the young fish emerge from the gravel the spring after hatching, they remain in their natal stream or an

adjacent lake for a year or more before swimming to salt water. After migrating and feeding for one to three years, they return to streams around the north Pacific Rim.

Throughout central and western Alaska, silvers are targeted by gillnetters and seiners. But like king salmon, cohos will eagerly strike a lure and have long been a target of trollers. Since the chinook season in Southeast Alaska was pared back, cohos are now the troll fleet's bread-and-butter fishery. Bled, cleaned and iced as soon as they come aboard, troll-caught cohos are among Alaska's premier salmon, with prices to match.

What attracts trollers to the coho also attracts sport fishermen, however, and silver salmon are one of the foremost sport fish in Alaska. In Bristol Bay and Cook Inlet, the Board of Fisheries has reduced commercial seasons to ensure good coho harvests for the state's other money-making fishing industry.

Cohos are not the only fish appreciated by both commercial and sport fishermen. Commercial seasons for sockeyes, chinooks and even chums have been cut throughout Alaska to provide more fish for anglers. The troll, seine and gillnet fleets argue that their industry was in place first — in some cases by a century — and wonder why they are being displaced by another. They suggest that Alaska's resident sport fishermen don't want or need more salmon, that the deductions from commercial catch are mostly for the benefit of lodge owners and sport fishing guides.

Though some Alaska anglers agree, others would be glad to have more fish snapping at their flies and lures. One group in the Matanuska-Susitna Borough sought to put a measure on the statewide ballot in 1996 that would have required ADF&G to manage Alaska's salmon fisheries so that 5 percent of the total statewide harvest would go to sport and personal-use fishermen — substantially more than the current level. Why should commercial fishermen get the lion's share of a public resource, they asked, leaving sport fishermen and guides the scraps?

The commercial fishing industry contested the measure, pointing out that sport fishermen would never take 5 percent of Bristol Bay sockeyes or Southeast pinks, and would therefore want the entire statewide salmon quota to come from the most accessible areas — Cook Inlet, Prince William Sound and Southeast. They claimed it would cripple the industry in some areas and kill it outright elsewhere.

Voters never got their say because a judge ruled that salmon allocation is

A few small skiffs are among the tools Alaska's sea-going State Troopers, the Division of Fish and Wildlife Protection, use to patrol areas such as the Egegik District of Bristol Bay. (Joel Gay)

a job for the Board of Fisheries, not Alaska voters.

But efforts to make more fish available to sport and personal use fishermen are likely to increase as numbers of both Alaska residents and tourists grow. Throughout the United States, commercial fisheries have come under attack in recent years for similar reasons — people don't want an industry to catch fish by the net-load when there aren't enough to catch by rod and reel. Legislatures and voters in California, Florida and Louisiana have set aside certain species for recreational harvest only, limited net fishing in some areas and banned it completely in others. At the same time, habitat destruction continues, pressuring reductions in commercial fishing to keep pace with declining stocks.

Governors, legislators, managers and special interest groups have said Alaska has enough fish for all, but

The F/V Lucy O *sets its seine while the F/V* Archangel *hauls one in near Sitka.* (Christian Racich)

argument will likely continue over the question, How much is enough? If the last 100 years are any indication, Alaska's salmon should endure the battle. Whether Alaska's 12,000 seiners, gillnetters and trollers survive is another question altogether. ◄

been, for a short time the *Fairtry* logged record-breaking catches. The good results did not last, though. The Soviet Union had caught wind of the vessel when it was still under construction and stolen a look at its plans. Before champagne ever flowed over the *Fairtry*, Soviet officials had placed an order with a West German shipbuilder for 24 copies. Within four years of the *Fairtry*'s launch, the USSR had two dozen just like it and 10 more even larger. By 1959 Soviet factory trawlers were fishing in the eastern Bering Sea.

They had company, however. Japanese trawlers had returned to Alaska waters a few years earlier, targeting fewer than 50 metric tons a year of groundfish and herring. The arrival of the Soviet factory trawlers coincided with — or perhaps spurred — a veritable arms race of fishing power between the two countries. By the time Korea and Poland entered the fishery in the 1970s, nearly 500 vessels hauled more than 2 million metric tons of groundfish annually out of the eastern Bering Sea and Gulf of Alaska. Japan caught three-fourths of it.

Pollock are one of several species, collectively known as groundfish, that make up the most valuable fishery in Alaska. Walleye or Pacific pollock typically grow to 18 inches, but they can reach 36 inches and are the dominant groundfish species in the Bering Sea. (Daryl Binney)

The catches did not go unnoticed, either in Alaska or Washington, D.C. Fishermen complained about foreign boats trawling off the shores of Kodiak and Sitka, and biologists watched helplessly as one stock after another plummeted due to overfishing. By 1971, Sen. Ted Stevens (R-Alaska) and Sen. Warren Magnuson (D-Wash.) began calling for an international version of limited entry — an Exclusive Economic Zone that would extend U.S. control of its coastal waters out to 200 miles.

It took five years, but in 1976 the idea won approval. Under what would eventually be known as the Magnuson-Stevens Fishery Management and Conservation Act, the United States started the process of "Americanization" — a euphemism for booting the foreign fleets out of the EEZ. With a stroke of his pen, President Gerald Ford created a quiet but powerful new cannon.

The Anchorage Hilton Hotel is where a fisherman now must go to fish the Bering Sea. Meeting there about five times a year, the North Pacific Fishery Management Council sits in judgment of all who would drop a net or longline in the federal waters off Alaska's coast. And many would like to try — the council controls fisheries

worth nearly $1 billion a year.

Though its decisions ultimately must win approval by the Secretary of Commerce, the council — and seven others like it managing the fish resources from Hawaii to Maine — has wide latitude to run its fisheries according to local preference.

Just as the Board of Fisheries quickly moved to eliminate fish traps, the North Pacific council jumped into Americanization with a vengeance. During the next 12 years of Hilton meetings the foreign fleets that caught nearly 100 percent of the fish in U.S. waters gradually lost their fishing rights as the council assigned more and more of the quota to domestic fishermen and processors.

Trawling was nothing new to Americans. Draggers, as the vessels are called when they deliver to shore plants, had worked off the East Coast and the Pacific Northwest for years by the time the Magnuson-Stevens Act was signed. But while fishermen and boats were ready to work, domestic processors had few markets for the fish. Joint ventures between American catcher boats and foreign processors proved to be the vital link.

The council paved the way by offering Japan, Korea and the other fishing nations continued access to American fish in exchange for their approval of joint-venture fisheries. "Magnuson called it the 'Fish and Chips Policy,'" said Clem Tillion, who was council chairman at the time. "'If you want a little fish, put some chips on the table.'"

Americanization had a parabolic growth curve once the first JV fishery broke the ice. Within five years American fishermen were catching nearly one-quarter of the North Pacific groundfish harvest. Within 12 years the last foreign vessel was gone, and while it was cause for celebration in the Hilton, the party didn't last long.

POLLOCK

The first time a civil war intruded on the Bering Sea was in 1865, when the Confederate cutter *Shenandoah* rounded up nearly two dozen Yankee whalers and burned them to the waterline over the issue of states' rights.

By the early 1990s, civil war had broken out again, this time over economics. For 15 years American fishermen had stood shoulder to shoulder and worked together to displace the

Workers feed headless pollock into a filleting machine at a shore-based surimi processor at Dutch Harbor. (Harry M. Walker)

Crewmen work with heavy machinery to haul in the huge trawl nets that fish wide swaths of the ocean. The efficiency of the trawlers accounted in part for the push in Congress to extend U.S. waters to 200 miles offshore in the 1970s. These efforts culminated in 1976 in the Magnuson-Stevens Fishery Management and Conservation Act, which increasingly limited foreign fishing within the 200-mile zone. (Daryl Binney)

foreign fleets. As their success became increasingly apparent, so did the competition over who would get the lion's share of the harvest — the factory trawler fleet or the joint venture boats and their processing partners, the shoreside plants in Dutch Harbor, Kodiak and elsewhere along the coast. The battle still rages.

The dispute centers on a soft, big-eyed fish called the walleye pollock. A member of the cod family, *Theragra chalcogramma* typically grows to 18 inches and 2 to 3 pounds. Pollock are thought to be the single most abundant fish in the world, inhabiting the entire North Pacific from Japan to California. The majority live in the Bering Sea.

Also called Alaska pollock, the fish are often filleted and frozen, but the majority are ground into a white, flavorless paste called surimi. It is the raw material for a wide range of products including artificial crab legs, lobster and shrimp, and a multitude

of foods in Japan known generally as *kamaboko*.

Japanese boats first targeted pollock in their own coastal waters in the 1950s. When surimi processing equipment became available in the mid-1960s, however, Japanese trawlers expanded into the Bering Sea. With other nations, the catch by 1976 was 5 million metric tons a year, making pollock the biggest single-species fishery on earth.

Americans had never shown much interest in groundfish, but it became a torrid love affair after the Magnuson-

Stevens Act promised them every fish within 200 miles of shore. Starting in 1976, more than $1 billion was invested in groundfish trawlers hoping to break into the lucrative pollock fishery. A few were built new, but most were converted from oil rig service ships, tankers, even sugar cane haulers. Eventually more than 70 factory trawlers came to ply the North Pacific, all flying the U.S. flag.

They were not the only Americans with eyes for pollock, however. Concurrent with the factory trawler boom was one on shore. Processing

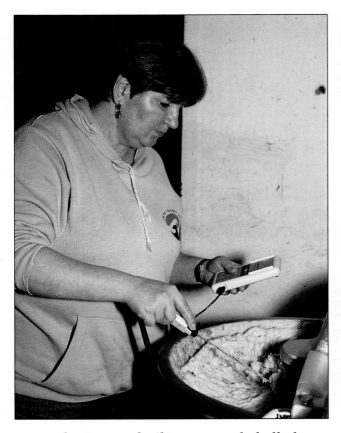

FAR LEFT: *A member of the quality control crew, Colleen Cornell tests the surimi being produced on board a factory trawler at sea. (Daryl Binney)*

LEFT: *Pollock is processed into a fish paste known as surimi, which can be molded into various shapes and is sometimes sold in grocery stores as artificial crab. (Daryl Binney)*

BELOW: *After it is processed, surimi is packed into flat loaves sometimes called "freezers" and frozen. This factory worker is breaking the "freezers" on board the* Arctic Storm *factory trawler. (Daryl Binney)*

plants were built or expanded all along the coast. Supplying them was the old joint venture fleet, with boats now capable of pulling the net on board and returning to port with 1 million pounds of fish in a refrigerated hold.

Even as the last of the foreign fishermen left, it was obvious there were too many American boats chasing too few fish. The pollock season shrank from 12 months a year to two. Factory trawlers had to find part-time work freezing and packaging salmon.

Some companies struck out for Russia, China and Antarctica. Others folded, selling vessels for a fraction of their value. The ships didn't revert to oil field service, however. They returned to the Bering Sea with different names and lower overhead, compounding the competition.

Clearly the factory trawlers could catch and process all the pollock in the North Pacific. That became painfully obvious to Kodiak-based shore plants and boats in the late 1980s. A fleet of

Bering Sea factory trawlers scooped up virtually the entire Gulf of Alaska pollock quota in a few days, leaving local plants and fishermen out of work. Calls arose to limit the factory trawlers' catch and to guarantee a share for shore plants, and while the calls began in Kodiak, they echoed loudly in Juneau and Anchorage.

Factory trawlers were incensed at the idea, saying it smacked of protectionism and socialism. The fish are American, not Alaskan, they pointed out, and argued that economics, not government agencies, should determine which sector of the fishing industry would survive the ultimate shakeout.

Shore plants and their supporters replied that the resource off Alaska's shore should provide jobs and tax revenue in Alaska, too, not just Washington. They likened the Seattle-based factory trawler fleet to the fish trap owners nearly a century before, and said the government was right to step in to provide a level playing field.

In 1991 the North Pacific council approved the idea, giving the shore plants and coastal trawlers 35 percent of the Bering Sea's pollock and 100 percent of the Gulf of Alaska quota, though the allocation was only supposed to last three years. In the

Packages of surimi are offloaded at Dutch Harbor. (Daryl Binney)

Automated jigging machines allow a small crew to seek out rockfish, lingcod and other species. A crew brings in rockfish, most likely shortraker rockfish. The fish on the deck are the same species: Rockfish darken as they age so the bright red fish is younger than the others. (Joel Gay)

meantime the council hoped to adopt a management strategy better than the current "Olympic" system, so called because participants race to catch the most fish before the quota is gone.

Several possible strategies emerged, and a few were enacted. The council called a moratorium on new entrants into the North Pacific fisheries, and limited vessel conversions to a size increase of 20 percent. The council set aside, however, the plan that many in the industry believed was the best way to rationalize the fisheries: individual fishing quotas, or IFQs.

Under an IFQ system, the quota of a given fishery would be divided among the vessel owners according to their vessels' historical percentage of the catch. The shares could be bought and sold, allowing smaller operators to increase their participation or sell out altogether. Proponents say economic pressure would cause the fleet to shrink, and would allow boats to take more time while harvesting, thus reducing waste.

Opponents argue that the vessel owners who stand to gain are mostly foreign corporations, and fear the further centralization of catching power in the hands of a few individuals or companies.

While the council approved IFQ programs for halibut and sablefish, and most industry observers expected the system would be extended to all groundfish and crab, the panel in 1995 balked at the idea. It may eventually adopt IFQs, but first it will put in place a license system making the pollock and cod fisheries much like Alaska salmon. The race continues.

ROCKFISH

Driving the 32-foot *Arctic Chinook* out of Seward one bright spring afternoon, it's hard to imagine a more idyllic workplace. Resurrection Bay is flat calm and whales' spouts punctuate the scenery. Glaciers pour around the sharp peaks of the Harding Icefield west of us like beer foaming through a broken bottle. Tourists pay top dollar for a visit to this staggering coastline and Kenai Fjords National Park.

Where mountains drop precipitously into the sea is rockfish territory. The skipper says we'll search around the gray granite pillars poking out of the Gulf of Alaska and along submerged ridges that extend off the mainland, targeting fish 150 feet deep. Less than a mile away the bottom drops more than 1,000 feet.

It's almost sundown by the time we reach No-Name Island, a 150-foot-high boulder that seems to have frozen as it leapt from the sea. The skipper slows the boat to an idle as the deckhand sets up the gear.

The *Arctic Chinook* will never be much competition for the factory trawler and freezer longliner fleet, but it too is reaping the rewards of Americanization, like hundreds of others owned and operated by coastal Alaska residents. Off the Yukon Delta they may fish for cod and halibut. But along the Aleutian Islands and throughout the Gulf of Alaska, the smallest of the state's groundfish fleets is busy much of the year chasing rockfish.

More than 50 species of rockfish inhabit the North Pacific. Slow-growing and long-lived, rockfish are particularly susceptible to overfishing — and many were when targeted by foreign trawlers in the 1960s and 1970s. Since 1976 conservation efforts have been put in place and now rockfish fishermen in Alaska have only themselves to compete with, using hooks, not nets.

As they have for more than a century, many fishermen use longlines for rockfish, and salmon fishermen in Southeast use trolling gear. But an increasingly popular method is jigging — dropping a hook on the ocean floor and raising and lowering it methodic-

One of the deck crew on a longliner always stands at the roller, ready to haul in the fish as they come up. (Art Sutch)

ally to attract the fish. Recreational fishermen jig for many species, including rockfish. Commercial fishermen became interested with the invention of jigging machines.

Any boat can be converted to jigging. Most fishermen put three to six machines around the deck rails. Each has a reel wound with heavy nylon or Kevlar line and a small electric or hydraulic motor. A cylindrical lead weight carries the line to the bottom. Half a dozen hooks are attached to

the line, one every fathom or so.

After dropping the weight and hooks overboard, we vector across a submerged ridge, pushed by wind and tide. "There's lots of circling, looking for fish, trying to figure out where you are," the skipper says as he stares into the depth sounder. The screen suggests our 18 hooks are sliding through a school of rockfish. The machines remain quiet, however.

Top-of-the-line jigging machines spool out until the sinker hits bottom, then reel in a set amount and begin jigging automatically. The operator can adjust all parameters, such as how far off the bottom to jig and the height of the jigging motion itself. They whir and hum and beep as they go through their paces.

The machines also sense when a fish hits, and when enough fish are hooked, they retract automatically, beeping all the way. After a long, quiet drift we reel up, expecting nothing. But the machines aren't infallible, and four black rockfish, *Sebastes melanops*, break the surface. Averaging 4 pounds apiece, they are heavily spined, dark gray on top and lighter on the bottom with big black eyes rimmed in gold — a noble-looking fish but for the pink air bladders popping out of their mouths. Like troll-caught salmon, the fish must be iced immediately and delivered every three to five days to ensure top quality.

Even taken together, the rockfishes sought by jig fishermen make up a tiny fraction of Alaska's groundfish fisheries. Other rockfish species, particularly the Pacific Ocean perch (*S. alatus*) are much more numerous, and were among the chief targets of foreign trawlers. But the king of the small-boat groundfish fisheries today is the same as it was 100 years ago, the Pacific cod.

PACIFIC COD

A woven cloth belt dangling below the waistband of his jacket and a long beard flowing over the top are dead giveaways that the skipper standing on the Homer dock is an Old Believer, a sect of the Russian Orthodox Church. Persecuted for clinging to their fundamentalist beliefs more than three centuries ago, many of the faithful fled east, to what is now Siberia. After the Bolshevik Revolution, fear of government repression again drove them on, this time into Manchuria. When Mao Tse-Tung took over the People's

Pacific cod await processing at Dutch Harbor. The shallow eastern Bering Sea, where the continental shelf extends out 400 miles or more, where the sea-bottom is relatively smooth and where there is an abundance of bottom- and midlevel-dwelling fish make ideal conditions for trawl fishing. (Harry M. Walker)

Crew members at St. Paul Island in the Pribilofs unload frozen cod for the trawler fleet. Since government subsidies were removed from the fur seal harvest in the early 1980s, the Pribilof Islanders have turned to other natural resources from the Bering Sea such as fish to sustain their economy. (Harry M. Walker)

Republic of China in 1949, those who could kept running, to Hong Kong, then South America, and eventually to Oregon. In 1968 a caravan of Old Believers drove up the Alaska Highway to carve a new town out of the wilderness north of Homer. They called it Nikolaevsk.

Tough and resourceful newcomers to a coastal community, the men turned to one of the few commercial opportunities at the time, fishing, and found it to their liking. Now, like most Alaska fishermen, salmon are the Old Believers' economic mainstay. But with salmon prices in the doldrums and many fishermen frozen out of the halibut fishery with the advent of individual fishing quotas, virtually any fish with even a modicum of value is a godsend.

So when the weather turned calm in late February, this Old Believer fired up his 40-foot boat, rounded up his crew and went in search of Alaska's original groundfish prey, Pacific cod. For years the fish was discarded as trash, or used only for bait in crab pots and on halibut hooks. But as Atlantic

cod stocks nosedived in the late 1980s, interest has boomed in Alaska's fish. Prices doubled, then doubled again for a few select markets. Competition is keen for the fish, not only on docks around the state but on the fishing grounds.

Once considered a pauper, the Pacific cod is now revealed to be a prince after all.

Also known as gray cod or "P. cod," *Gadus macrocephalus* span the full spectrum of Alaska's groundfish fleets. Targeted by factory trawlers and 32-footers, fished from the Pribilof Islands to Petersburg, the fish are caught with trawls, longlines, pots and hooks. The

catch typically tops 300,000 metric tons per year, making Pacific cod second only to pollock in landings.

Far to the west, in a warehouse in Dutch Harbor, workers shovel salt onto piles of cod trawled off the bottom of the Bering Sea. These fish are bound for Portugal, long one of the major markets for cod. Portuguese vessels, along with Spanish, Canadian, Russian and others, throttled the cod business in the North Atlantic by overfishing in the 1970s. After years of high-level harvesting, the supply itself dried up.

Because the North Atlantic was so bounteous, however, foreign vessels virtually ignored the North Pacific

Longline gear is baited with squid to go after groundfish, most likely Pacific cod. (Harry M. Walker)

until after the United States enacted its 200-mile limit. Now Alaska trawlers supply much of the cod consumed in the U.S., and the majority comes from the Bering Sea.

Cod spend most of their lives on the ocean floor, growing as big as 30 pounds but often in the 8- to15-pound range. They have what is known as a strong "gulp reflex," which means that whatever happens to enter their mouth is promptly swallowed — from juvenile king crab to adult pollock. Studies of their stomach contents suggest cod may be responsible for decimating stocks of crab, shrimp, herring and other fish in certain areas.

That innate hunger is also what makes Pacific cod an easy target for small-boat fishermen. Though they cannot trawl, these boats in the 32- to 60-foot range can drop pots and longlines and haul up the fish a few at a time. In towns all around the Gulf of Alaska, cod has become a fall, winter and spring fishery that increasing numbers of fishermen rely on.

Many use their halibut longlines, though with smaller hooks. Veteran skippers say they almost always caught cod while chasing the bigger, more lucrative halibut, but never kept them. Now they're worth enough to bring back. And finding them is easy, says

the Old Believer on the Homer dock. "If you fish for halibut, you know where to go."

Longliners are not the only ones getting double duty out of their gear. Crab fishing has fallen on hard times in recent years, too, and idle crabbers in Kodiak, Homer and elsewhere began cod fishing with pots in the late 1980s. A cod smells the bait inside and can't resist. Bright orange nylon "cod triggers" lashed into the pot's mouth act like the dragon's teeth in a drive-in movie, allowing the fish in but not out.

"It was a matter of opportunity," said ADF&G biologist Bill Nippes in Kodiak. "The gear was already here. There were declining stocks elsewhere, and we had boats looking for things to do."

The Gulf of Alaska has a much smaller cod quota than the Bering Sea, and it too was traditionally caught by trawlers. But when pot and longline fishermen entered the fishery in full force, they took almost one-quarter.

Their success prompted a group of small-boat fishermen to ask the Alaska Board of Fisheries to open a separate cod fishery in state waters every year after the federal fishery closes. The board agreed, extracting another 15 percent of the Gulf of Alaska quota from the big boats. Only pot and jig fishermen are allowed in the new fishery, however, because longliners targeting Pacific cod inevitably catch halibut.

Fisheries managers are increasingly concerned about the incidental catch of other species. When a bottom trawl drags across the sea bed, it catches not only cod, but coral, plants, crab and other species of fish. When a longliner or jig fisherman drops a baited hook, there is no guarantee what fish will bite. Even pot fishermen catch the wrong size, sex and species of crab and in the process of throwing them back occasionally kill them. For many fisheries, that incidental catch has become as important as the target catch itself.

FLATFISH

Trawl fishermen around the world tell stories about the strange assortment of goods they have hauled up in their nets. Bathtubs, torpedoes, human cadavers, cases of wine, even old school buses have surfaced. Trawlers have netted submarines, and one California skipper reported landing an Air Force

Fishing and seafood processing provide the bulk of the economy for King Cove, on the Pacific side of the Alaska Peninsula 18 miles southeast of Cold Bay. King Cove is home to Peter Pan Seafoods, among the largest seafood processing facilities under one roof in the country. (Art Sutch)

guided missile. The Air Force got it back, though not before agreeing to pay for the fisherman's damaged gear.

Any unintended or unwanted booty is called bycatch, and while some has a humorous aspect, American groundfish fishermen have amassed a substantial amount of unwelcome bycatch since taking over the North Pacific. Almost every year, trawlers, longliners, pot and jig fishermen discard nearly 750 million pounds of fish because it is the wrong size, sex or species. Trawlers account for more than 80 percent of it.

No fishery is immune to bycatch problems. But the North Pacific discards have come under intense scrutiny from several powerful quarters, including Congress, and the North Pacific council is under strict orders to reduce it.

Not surprisingly, the "dirtiest" fisheries target roe, particularly of the flatfish, an entire order (*Pleuronectiformes*) that has adapted to a life spent on the ocean floor, with eyes on the top of the head and the mouth on the bottom. These include the soles, halibut and flounders, as well as many lesser species. Taken together, the "flats" are the most numerous fish in the North Pacific. Unfortunately for fishermen, the most numerous of all, the arrowtooth flounder (*Atheresthes*

A crewman shows off a large sablefish caught in Southeast waters. (Art Sutch)

stomias), is rendered almost inedible during processing, and most other flatfish are too small to fillet. A few select species, however, are valued simply for their roe.

Though the flesh of both yellowfin sole (*Limanda aspera*) and rock sole (*Lepidopsetta bilineata*) is highly regarded and valuable in its own right, a fleet of some two dozen Bering Sea trawlers fish during the winter when the roe content is highest. Because it doesn't pay to fill their holds with anything less valuable than roe-bearing females, most other fish, including males, are thrown overboard.

In a typical rock sole roe season, more than 3 metric tons of cod, pollock, halibut and male rock sole are discarded for every ton of females retained. The fleet kills and discards more than 430,000 juvenile halibut, 100,000 king crab and 3 million tanner crab.

Proponents of the industry argue that the waste has a higher purpose. In two months the fleet will earn upwards of $50 million, making rock sole one of the most lucrative fisheries in the North Pacific. Most of the discarded fish are worth far less, they say, and note that maximizing the value of the fisheries is one of the goals of the Magnuson-Stevens Act. Because the council takes the waste of each species into account when setting quotas, it isn't a conservation problem —the fish will be caught in one fishery or another. The issue, they say, boils down to the question of who eats them — humans, or scavengers on the floor of the Bering Sea?

Opponents argue that there are far better uses of the discarded fish. Killing a 1-pound juvenile halibut robs some fisherman in the future of a 30- or 60- or 200-pound adult fish. They maintain that the world's oceans cannot and should not have to support wasteful fishing practices, and that if humans aren't going to eat the fish, fishermen should leave them alone.

The other big bottom trawl fishery, Pacific cod, has similar discard rates. Both factory trawlers and shore-based draggers discard almost 50 percent of their catch, including a substantial amount of cod.

Pollock, on the other hand, has a surprisingly low discard rate. Most are caught in "midwater trawls" — the net is towed fast enough that it stays off the bottom. Throughout the mid-1990s, only 4 percent was discarded, though 4 percent of nearly 3 billion pounds is still a substantial figure.

The North Pacific council has been grappling with bycatch issues since 1976. Among the first regulations it enacted were bycatch caps on the most profitable species, halibut, salmon, herring and crab. It also put observers on the foreign vessels to keep track of their catches. As soon as a particular fishery reached its bycatch limit, fishing stopped.

As Americans took over individual fisheries, bycatch issues became even more sensitive. They didn't have as much fishing experience in the North Pacific and bycatch rates in some fisheries jumped. Trawlers took the brunt of the complaints, but longliners, too, have been singled out for catching too many of the wrong species, especially halibut.

Under pressure from Congress, environmental groups and the industry

SABLEFISH

One of the most valuable species in Alaska has perhaps the most names. The long, thin, dark gray animal that Japanese consumers call "butterfish" for its delicate and tasty flesh, that scientists know as *Anoplopoma fimbria* and that managers designate "sablefish," is known to fishermen throughout Alaska as blackcod.

Not a true cod at all, sablefish are deep-water denizens found from Baja California to the Bering Sea, though the largest concentrations are in the Gulf of Alaska. They typically grow to about 3 feet and 7 pounds. Sablefish have an oily flesh that does not cook well. The Japanese prefer the flesh raw, as *sashimi*, while many North Americans like it smoked.

Nevertheless, sablefish often fetch twice as much per pound as halibut and are at least a dozen times more valuable than Pacific cod. Alas, sablefish are found in smaller numbers, with the annual catch from all Alaska waters typically around 30 million pounds (compared to 600 million pounds of Pacific cod, for example.)

Sablefish fishing is relatively new to the North Pacific, and traditionally done with hook and line. Since many of the same boats that fished halibut also fished blackcod, the North Pacific Fishery Management Council simultaneously considered and approved both fisheries for IFQs.

While the vast majority of sablefish are caught in federal waters in a season that lasts from March to November, several fisheries closer to shore are managed by ADF&G. The granddaddy of them all is in Chatham Strait, in Southeast, where the fishery developed into one of the wildest 24-hour derbies in the state. At its peak, the fleet of 120 boats each set an average of one hook per second for eight straight hours. Some boats caught as much as 60,000 pounds in that one long day.

While the fleet size had been limited years earlier, biologists were concerned about the health of the stocks because fishermen were using larger boats and more gear. In 1994 the Board of Fisheries adopted a radical new management plan for Chatham Strait that gave each permit holder an equal share of the quota. The top fishermen were

furious, but most of the fleet approves of the kinder, gentler fishery.

Humans are not alone in their love for sablefish. Longliners working in Prince William Sound and off the Aleutian Islands occasionally find killer whales picking the fish right off their hooks as the lines are retrieved. They have tried all sorts of measures to scare the whales away, but the only successful way to protect their catch has been to move to new grounds. ◄

Sablefish, or blackcod, are often the most valuable fish longliners catch and a big load can make a good payday. This crew is unloading its catch at Pelican in Southeast. (Art Sutch)

itself, the council in 1995 began working on a plan to drastically reduce bycatch. The first phase, to be implemented in 1998, will require all Bering Sea vessels to retain 100 percent of the pollock and Pacific cod they bring on board. That measure alone should reduce discards by 50 percent. The flatfish fisheries are next, but will have five years to develop new markets. A parallel program is being developed for the Gulf of Alaska.

Bycatch has proven to be one of the most difficult problems for the fishing industry to rein in, because every fish that goes overboard allows another fish to be caught or kept. But Congress made it clear, when it reauthorized the Magnuson-Stevens Act in 1997, that the North Pacific, big as it is, is not big enough to waste. ◄

HALIBUT

Torrential rain and storm-force wind blast the tarmac at the Coast Guard air station on a typical fall night in Kodiak, inscribing a wet, gray aurora on the concrete. Inside one of the huge hangars four helicopters sit smug and dry, their white-and-orange skins gleaming in bright counterpoint to the liquid dark outdoors.

Across the street in Ready Crew Berthing a dozen young fliers lounge around, playing cards, watching videos and waiting for the alarm that will send one of their aircraft into the foul night. They are surprisingly nonchalant considering that the next phone call might demand they search the stormy Gulf of Alaska for a capsized boat or tiny life raft, or pull a fisherman's lifeless body off a lonesome gravel beach.

But chances are good no call will come tonight. Though halibut prices are high these days and many longliners have ventured into the Gulf, the boats have either returned to port or are safely anchored in remote coves to wait out the storm.

It's a dramatic turnabout for Air Station Kodiak, where flight crews just a few years earlier had come to dread halibut openings. So many fishermen had turned to halibut for extra income that the season length was cut and cut again until the entire Gulf of Alaska quota — more than three-fourths of all halibut caught in the Pacific — was landed in as little as 48 hours. Opening dates were set months in advance and held regardless of the weather. Boat sinkings were common and scores of fishermen died. It was a rare opening when the helicopters did not fly.

Yet changing the management system proved to be perhaps the stormiest issue in the history of the North Pacific fisheries. Of several possible alternatives, the concept that rose to the surface would not only limit the size of the fleet, as with salmon, but also limit each fisherman's catch through individual quotas. They could buy more quota, and they could fish whenever they wanted. But under "individual fishing quotas," or IFQs, never again could they catch as much as luck allowed.

It took years of wrangling before IFQs were approved, but after the first season in 1995, many halibut fishermen breathed a sigh of relief.

FACING PAGE: *Another hold full of halibut is unloaded at Homer. Halibut spawn in deep water where prolific females have been known to produce more than 2 million eggs. Eggs and larvae drift with the currents. When the larvae are less than 1 inch long, the eye on the blind side begins to move to the eyed side. When they are 3 to 4 inches long, the larvae settle to the bottom, usually far from where they were spawned. (Chlaus Lotscher)*

"It reminds me of the old days," said one veteran longliner, "when we fished when we wanted to, not when we were told to."

The Pacific halibut holds nearly as venerable a place in the North Pacific fisheries as the chinook salmon, having been one of the chief species sought by Natives as well as one of the first chased by commercial fishermen. Halibut, too, can grow to monstrous proportions — an angler in Unalaska reeled in a 459-pounder recently — and can live to 40 years or more. No matter how they are prepared, halibut are considered by many the tastiest fish in the sea.

When hatched, the free-floating larvae of *Hippoglossus stenolepis* look like most other fish, with one eye on each side of its body. By the time they reach an inch, however, the body has flattened and the left eye has migrated to the top. At six months the fish settle to the bottom, though they continue to roam the rest of their lives. Juveniles tagged along the Aleutian Islands have been caught as adults off Oregon.

Halibut spend their winters at depths to 1,500 feet but migrate close to shore every summer, and Natives from central California to the Bering Sea caught them using fiber lines and hooks of wood or bone. Some fished out of canoes and kayaks while others set a baited hook at one low tide and retrieved a fish during the next.

Commercial salmon fishermen delivering to Alaska's first cannery in Klawock in 1878 also brought in some of the huge flatfish, though canned halibut never developed much of a following. The landmark event in the fishery occurred in 1888 when the sailing ship *Oscar and Hattie* caught 50,000 pounds of halibut off British Columbia, packed it in ice and sent the load to Boston on the just-completed Northern Pacific Railroad.

Railroad cars were almost as important as fishing boats to the new industry, as West Coast markets were meager. Without ice, however,

FAR LEFT: *Many consider halibut the tastiest fish in the ocean. The largest of the flatfish, Pacific halibut followed their cousin, the Atlantic halibut, in becoming an important food when processors and fishermen learned how to transport Pacific halibut to the East Coast market. (Art Sutch)*

LEFT: *A cannery worker stacks frozen halibut at Icicle Seafoods, Petersburg. (Karen Cornelius)*

the trans-continental shipments were doomed, and when none was available around Puget Sound, boats went as far north as Glacier Bay to chip it out of Alaska icefields.

In its infancy, the halibut fleet comprised no more than 20 coal- or oil-fired steamships, each with a flock of small dories on deck and a crew of 20 and more. Every day the dorymen dropped hemp or manila lines up to 2,000 feet long and bristling with more than 200 hooks baited with octopus or cod. Fishing on virgin grounds, the steamships logged phenomenal success. Many boats landed 1 million pounds a year and the market clamored for more.

Despite their profitability, they were labor intensive operations. Mother-ships carried as many as 14 dories, each of which required two fishermen. As crewmen unionized for higher pay and better working conditions, the owners looked elsewhere — to schooners— to lower their costs. Smaller and cheaper to build and run, schooners were well-suited to the conditions farther offshore, where fishing had to move after near-shore stocks were depleted. And best of all for owners, the longline gear could be fished directly off the deck, eliminating the need for dories. The first schooners appeared on the grounds around 1915 and by 1930 the steamship era was over.

Even as schooners displaced the "smoke boats," however, their own future was cloudy. A new breed of

Halibut are cleaned at sea and their gut cavity, or poke, is filled with ice. (Art Sutch)

fisherman was becoming increasingly common all along the Pacific coast, the independent operator. In Alaska, these were salmon fishermen who needed boats that could fish for halibut during the fall and winter, herring in the spring, and cod, crab or any other species for which there were buyers. They called the new craft "combination boats," and with them Alaska's modern, diversified coastal fishing industry was born. Salmon may have been the fleet's mainstay, but the huge, white-bellied halibut have played a key role in their success to date.

Like the calm eye in the center of a storm, a pair of biologists in matching yellow rain gear and blue baseball caps seem to be studying a halibut laid out on a table on the Kodiak waterfront. All around them is the buzz of activity — cannery foremen yell orders over the din, bulging netloads of fish rise out of boat holds and drip gurry on the workers below, forklifts carry thousand-pound totes into the processing plants like insects returning to their hive.

One of the biologists weighs and measures the fish before him, then slices into the head of one fish with a scalpel. Using a stout pair of tweezers, she extracts the otolith — a small, white, shell-like growth from its inner

ear — and deposits it in a numbered specimen jar. After recording length, weight and the otolith number, this halibut joins the rest coming across the dock today. In a few hours it will be clean, frozen and ready for market.

In a few months, however, the staff of the International Pacific Halibut Commission will cut the otolith in half, inspect it under a microscope and determine the age of the fish by reading the number of growth rings it

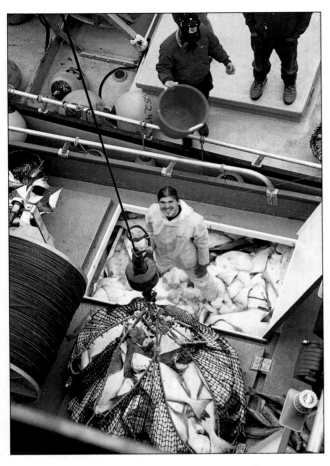

FAR LEFT: *This fisherman is glad to be back in port, with a big load of halibut to boot.* (Joel Gay)

LEFT: *Biologists with the International Pacific Halibut Commission pluck the otolith, or ear bone, out of several thousand halibut every year to better understand the life history of the fish and make good management decisions.* (Joel Gay)

shows. Comparing its age with its length, weight and other factors gleaned from the skipper who caught it will provide another small clue about the size and health of halibut stocks of the North Pacific.

Even in the pioneer days of the fishery, Americans were never alone on the halibut grounds. Fully half the steamship fleet was Canadian, and British Columbia ports were as busy as those of Washington and Alaska.

Boats from both nations fished the same grounds, and as early as 1900 recognized the first signs of depletion, smaller fish and lower catches. They didn't know much about *Hippoglossus,* but they knew that if fishing continued throughout the winter spawning season, their future was bleak.

Conservation was a hard sell on both sides of the border, but a steep decline in catches after World War I spurred the two countries to sign the Halibut Convention of 1923. It mandated a three-month closed period every winter, and installed a commission of two Americans and two Canadians to manage both the harvest

and conservation of halibut off the North American coast.

As time passed, the panel was renamed the International Pacific Halibut Commission and earned broader authority over stocks from California to the Bering Sea. It banned trawls, dories and fishing in nursery areas. The commission also started a research program that provided valuable information about the early life, migration, spawning and other details of halibut life. It took several decades, but under the agency's watchful eye the halibut stocks eventually rebounded.

Just as stocks peaked, however, a new threat appeared on the horizon. In the early 1960s foreign vessels started bottom trawling in the Bering Sea and Gulf of Alaska. Though their targets were pollock, sole and other groundfish, they scooped up millions of pounds of halibut. No one knows the exact figure because the trawlers neither carried observers nor reported their take, but estimates put the incidental halibut catch at 25 million pounds in some years — 25 million pounds that the IPHC was compelled to take away from American and Canadian fishermen to maintain the health of the fishery.

Since the trawlers were not fishing specifically for halibut, they were exempt from IPHC authority. As the trawl bycatch continued unabated through the early 1970s, North American longliners' harvests fell to the lowest levels since the fishery began. Halibut bycatch was one of many incendiary issues that prompted both Canada and the United States to declare 200-mile limits in the mid-1970s.

With the newly formed North Pacific Fishery Management Council breathing down their necks in 1977, the trawlers of Japan, the Soviet Union and other nations had no choice but to reduce their halibut bycatch. The stocks rebounded with gusto.

Quotas soared, too, attracting a steady stream of new participants into the fishery. As early as 1978 the council pondered ways to limit the halibut fleet. In 1983 a council plan to stem the flood of new boats and fishermen was shot down by the Reagan Administration, however, which disapproved of any limits that

did not also include some means of selling the fishing privileges.

The setback in limited entry planning was only momentary because the fleet was growing far faster than the halibut population. From 1977 to 1987, the Gulf of Alaska catch more than doubled, from about 20 million pounds to nearly 50 million, yet the season had dropped from 43 days to three 24-hour periods. Fishermen and managers stopped calling it the North Pacific halibut fishery. It had become, simply, the Derby.

For a typical halibut derby opening, fishermen from Wrangell to Sand Point loaded their boats with food, fuel and ice and made for the offshore fishing grounds a day or two early. The fleet included a number of year-round longliners who also fished for Pacific cod, sablefish and perhaps rockfish, as well as salmon and crab fishermen whose boats were easily modified to fish with longline gear.

Joining the professionals were "weekend warriors," fishermen with little or no commercial experience

Homer is one of the top halibut ports in the North Pacific, usually second only to Kodiak in total landings. (Joel Gay)

fishing out of pleasure boats. Limited entry was in the air and because the system would be based on historical participation, some boats fished simply out of speculation they might reap some reward in the future. At its peak the halibut fleet numbered more than 5,000 vessels, ranging from skiffs to 150-foot freezer-longliners.

Regardless of size, they all shared

This commercial halibut crew has a good catch off Afognak Island near Kodiak. (James L. Davis)

the hope that they might come home with a full hold. With just 24 hours to fish, a boat was either lucky or not when it began setting its gear. If not, the lines and hooks were easily recovered. If fishing was good, a 36-foot boat might pull aboard 25,000 pounds. For a few boats, however, the harvest was too good. Every year several million pounds of halibut were abandoned because the skipper didn't have time to retrieve them all. The longlines were simply cut and deserted, eventually balling up into a tangle of nylon and steel.

During a derby opener it was not uncommon for fishermen to work 30 or more hours without sleep, and more than one skipper fell asleep at the wheel and ran his boat onto the rocks after a halibut opening. Even when weather was good, minor emergencies were expected. The combination of hooks, knives, fish weighing 50 to 100 pounds and exhausted crews was a recipe for medical emergencies. When storms came up with little notice, the results could be tragic.

State and federal enforcement officials in boats, helicopters and airplanes tried their best to ensure nobody fished early or late and occasionally caught vessels with their gear in the water.

With nearly 1 million square miles of ocean to patrol, there was little doubt that cheating occurred, however.

Back on shore, the processing plants prepared for the derbies by hiring extra workers and paying overtime to handle the flood of fish. For a few days the markets from Anchorage to Miami offered fresh halibut, but the bulk of the catch was frozen.

The council considered several options for resolving the derby dilemma, but only one, individual fishing quotas, seemed up to the task. Splitting the quota among fishermen would allow them to sit out the storms, fish more carefully and eliminate wastage, and put fresh fish on the market eight months a year. The quota shares would be transferable, allowing the fleet size to shrink but also allowing new fishermen to buy their way in. The most challenging aspect of the IFQ proposal was deciding who should get the initial allocation. Boat owners? Skippers? Investors? Crew members?

Talk of IFQs had started as early as 1978, and it rose to the surface again after the limited entry idea was quashed. Fishermen, processors, even city councils all around the Gulf of Alaska weighed in with their opinions. Proponents called the overhaul long overdue, and even proposed that IFQs be applied to all fisheries in the North Pacific. Opponents said the cure was worse than the sickness. They feared that small, Alaska-based boats would

Alaska commercial fishermen caught about $77 million worth of halibut in 1996. These fish are headed for Icicle Seafoods at Petersburg. (Karen Cornelius)

gradually sell out to large, Seattle-based operations and that Alaska would lose not only its fleet but the lifeblood of its coastal towns. They vowed to fight the proposal all the way to the U.S. Supreme Court, and did after IFQs won final approval in January 1993.

In the end the council gave the quota shares to the vessel owners, based on their boats' catch records in the late 1980s. Some fishermen became millionaires overnight, and some lost their jobs. A few boat owners who never fished got rich while their hired skippers got nothing. Crew members were left out entirely, though they, too, are entitled to buy shares.

The vast majority of IFQ recipients, however, were owner-operators living in Alaska. Now that they have a guaranteed share of the quota, some of the adventure of halibut fishing has been lost. In return, they have a more stable industry. Prices have risen because the maximum amount of fish is now sold fresh, the level of financial risk has fallen because a boat knows how much fish it can catch in a given year, and on stormy nights when gales rake the Gulf of Alaska they can wait until the weather clears to set their hooks for the mighty Pacific halibut. ◄

ENVIRONMENT

Why is it that Alaska salmon stocks are booming while many in the Pacific Northwest are on the verge of extinction, and why are Steller sea lion stocks in just the opposite condition? Where did Kodiak's shrimp go, what makes salmon smaller now than 20 years ago, and who knows when the king crab will return to Kachemak Bay?

No one has the answers, but biologists worldwide are beginning to peek into the black box of ocean ecology, where global environmental conditions meld to affect everything from the tiniest zooplankton and the great blue whales to tides, currents and the jet stream. To date they have more questions than answers, but increasingly the scientific community is applying a broad, ecosystem approach in its quest to understand what makes the water planet work.

The information they have gleaned so far is fascinating, yet offers only a glimpse of how much more there is to learn. For example, marine biologists noted a sudden warming of the

Gulf of Alaska around 1977. By correlating water temperatures taken during the years by biologists with air temperature records kept by Russian Orthodox priests in Sitka for nearly 200 years, scientists believe they have found evidence that the Gulf undergoes a "regime shift" every 19 years or so, regularly warming or cooling by some 2 degrees C.

Judging from the good

catches of crab and shrimp, crustaceans apparently benefited from the colder temperatures of the 1960s and 1970s, while Alaska salmon fared poorly. Conversely, since the warm regime hit, Alaska salmon have been on a record run while many shellfish species have dwindled.

At the same time, it appears that salmon throughout the North Pacific are smaller than their forebears of 20 years earlier. And while some shellfish stocks are in the dumps, others appear to be plugging along as usual.

Biologists are also at a loss to explain why only western Alaska stocks of Steller sea lions have declined when their cousins in Washington, Oregon

and California prosper. Even though commercial fishing has been pared back in the Bering Sea and Gulf of Alaska, westward sea lion numbers continue to drop, leading many biologists to conclude that fishing may play a role, but perhaps not the lead role.

If the regime shift is linked to sea lion starvation, clues could come from predator-prey research underway elsewhere in Alaska. Scientists in the 1980s discovered that the zooplankton in any given area share a unique

LEFT: *ADF&G biologist Arnie Shaul is surrounded by paperwork, charts and radios as he manages the complex salmon fishery commonly known as "False Pass," and officially known as Area M. (Joel Gay)*

FACING PAGE: *A DeHaviland Beaver floatplane visits a purse seiner fishing in lower Cook Inlet. Modern fisheries have adopted the latest in equipment, gear and transportation to remain competitive. In some cases, these improvements have enabled fishermen to bring in substantial catches while having less effect on the ocean bottom or on non-target species. But more efficient gear can lead to rapid overfishing and managers need to carefully assess the stocks to ensure that the species can replenish itself. (Harry M. Walker)*

ratio of carbon and nitrogen isotopes, and the exact ratio reappears in every animal that eats them. Now biologists can trace where an animal has been by determining what it has eaten, much like they can tell past weather from the thickness of tree rings.

Research biologists in British Columbia have used the isotope method to trace salmon migration in hopes of learning more about a truly global issue — the carrying capacity of the North Pacific. Is there a limit to how many salmon the ocean can support? Can the massive hatcheries in Alaska, Japan and Russia pump out increasing numbers of salmon? Those questions have yet to be answered, but already the effort to answer them has shed light on why run sizes vary every year.

Other research has shown that periodic shifts in water temperature are typical and that fish populations rise and fall with regularity — the proof is in the mud. By taking core samples of shallow bays from California to Alaska and reading the thickness of layers of scales, biologists have documented the changing abundance of schooling fishes, sardines, anchovies and herring.

Ecosystem studies are underway in Prince William Sound and San Diego, the Bering Sea and the Sea of Japan, and though the scientific community throughout the North Pacific is making steady progress, the ocean has yet to give up all its secrets. Together, however, biologists eventually may get a good look at what goes on inside the black box. Fishermen can hardly wait. ◄

KING AND TANNER CRAB

The storm strikes with little warning, though they often do on the crab fishing grounds of the Bering Sea. The boat, 125 feet of hard steel and a veteran of a dozen seasons, bounces like a cork, dwarfed by green waves that break hard on its bow and wash across its deck.

The skipper knows this weather all too well, and though it takes work to keep the vessel headed into the wind, he expects to ride it out. The deckhands, armed with baseball bats, take turns breaking the ice that steadily collects on the rigging and rails and makes the boat top-heavy. They hate the unrelenting rise and fall of the bow and the shuddering thud of the sea. But they put up with it because yesterday they each made $1,000 before breakfast, and they will again tomorrow, or as soon as this storm passes.

Then something happens. No one will ever know why, but the vessel develops a list, or the stern begins to sink. As the skipper struggles with the helm, the next big wave blasts out a wheelhouse window. Another knocks the boat on its side. It rolls upright, but too slowly, and another wave lays it over again. The engine dies. The power is out. In the darkness and confusion the deckhands scramble for survival suits. Someone releases the life raft, but it catches in the rigging. The crew numbly wrestles with it in howling winds and blinding spray, getting in just as the boat — their home, protector, wealth and warmth — heaves one last time, then slips into the sea.

Commercial fishing is by far the most dangerous occupation in the United States, but Alaska's wintertime crab fisheries make salmon and herring fisheries look positively benign. In their heyday, the king crab boats fishing the Bering Sea and Gulf of Alaska were the deadliest workplaces in America, killing and maiming dozens of skippers and crew members every year. On a single grim day in 1983 two crabbers sank without a trace, taking 14 lives. Within a month the death toll in that fishery was nearly 20, and by year's end 30 crab fishermen had been lost to the cold, gray depths of the North Pacific.

Not surprisingly, the region was also one of the richest workplaces in the country, perhaps in the world. Deckhands on some boats earned $100,000 or more in a few weeks and often spent thousands in a single night

FACING PAGE: *A load of red king crab aboard the F/V* Bering Sea *is being delivered to Royal Aleutian Seafoods in Dutch Harbor. King crab were the foundation of Alaska's lucrative crab industry until stocks collapsed in the early 1980s. (Dan Parrett)*

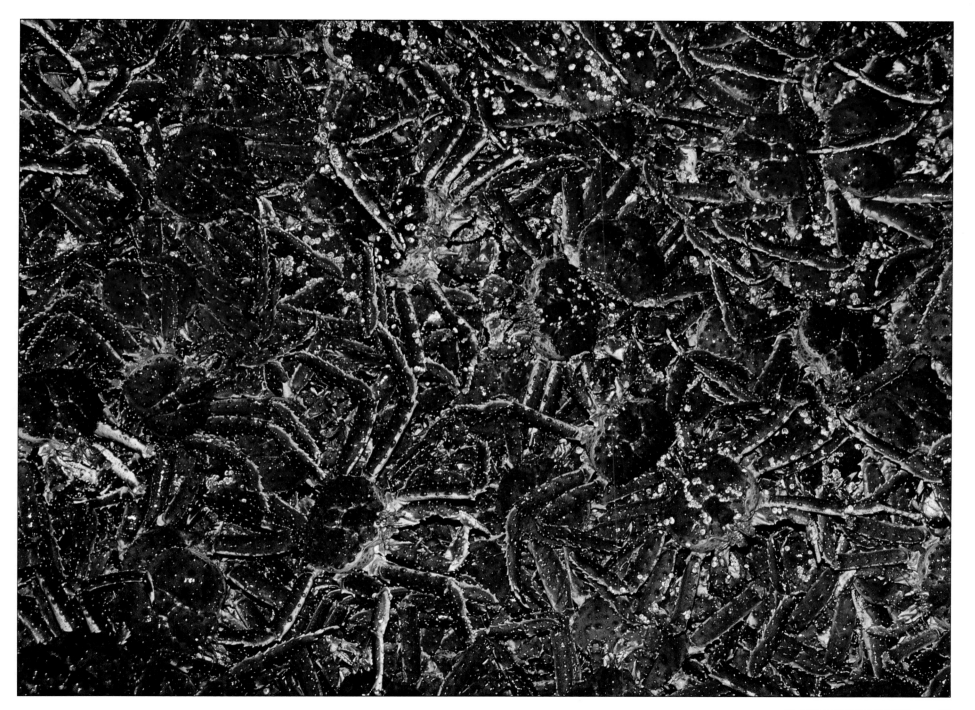

Cook Inlet, Kodiak and the Alaska Peninsula starting in the 1920s, and the first king crab cannery in the United States opened in Seldovia in 1923. But catches and canning were limited until a visionary Kodiak processor named Lowell Wakefield accidentally stumbled on an even better process for preserving the big crab, freezing. His marketing efforts boosted king crab sales throughout the country. To feed the demand, Wakefield built the first catcher-processor — a trawler on which the crab were butchered, cooked and frozen.

The domestic fishery was humbled after 1959 when the new state of Alaska banned tangle nets and, shortly thereafter, trawls. The conservation-minded Board of Fisheries said nets killed too many female and undersized crab. The practical effect of the prohibition, however, was to reduce competition for the state's fledgling small-boat fleet that fished with pots.

Alaska fishermen had found the traditional round pots used by Dungeness crabbers in the Lower 48 too light for the North Pacific, and with customary Alaska ingenuity invented their own. The first were

out back on shore. Million-dollar vessels were paid off in a single season, and hundreds of millions were invested in boats, processing plants and the pots that caught the focus of all the attention: red king crab.

Paralithodes camtschatica has long been considered the crème de la crème of Alaska's crustaceans. It can grow to 25 pounds with a leg span greater than 6 feet, though the average crab typically weighs about 6 pounds. Red king crab are found along most of Alaska's coast, as are their slightly smaller and less numerous cousins,

the blue (*P. platypus*) and brown or golden (*Lithodes aequispina*) king crab.

As with groundfish, the first to target king crab extensively were Japanese vessels, which fished the Bering Sea from the late 1800s to World War II and resumed in the mid-1950s. Trawlers dragged crab off the bottom; a fleet of small boats used tangle nets — long, shallow nets similar to gillnets, with glass floats along the top but weighted so heavily that they sank to the bottom. They snagged the crab by their spines and feet.

American boats had fished around

welded out of Army cots. As time passed, the pots gradually increased in size to 8 feet square and 3 feet deep with a weight of 800 pounds.

As demand increased and crab prices crept upward in the 1960s, so too did fishermen's wages. Some young deckhands earned $50,000 a year at a time their peers in San Francisco were tuning in, turning on and dropping out. Though the work was hard and the seasons long and cold, word spread in the fishing community that big money was being made, and soon the first steel boat was built specifically for crabbing. The 99-foot, Kodiak-based *Peggy Jo* was stouter, could withstand worse weather, fish farther out and carry more pots than most of its competition. Its advantage was short-lived, however.

By 1971, boatyards from Puget Sound to the Gulf of Mexico were working overtime to keep up with the demand for new steel crabbers. It cost $100,000 or more just to get on the list for a Marco 94-footer, but those who got the sturdy new vessels were reward-ed handsomely, fishing for red, brown and blue king crab from Kodiak to St. Matthew Island nearly year-round.

A blue king crab, caught near St. Matthew Island in the Bering Sea, is delivered to the processor Blue Wave. *This species is slightly smaller and less numerous than red king crab.* (Daryl Binney)

The granddaddy of all fisheries, however, was Bristol Bay. By the late 1960s catches had dropped off around Kodiak and the Alaska Peninsula, and as fishermen built tougher boats capable of withstanding the weather, they began to concentrate their effort in the eastern Bering Sea. The fishery seemed to defy all the norms of fishing. Even as the fleet size gradually increased, the quota virtually exploded, and the average boat's catch quadrupled from 1968 to 1978. Prices rose, too, from 38 cents a pound to $1.23 in four years.

The only aspect of the fishery that declined was the season length, which fell from three months to six weeks. Fishermen often worked 24, 30, even 40 hours straight when they were "on the crab," sleeping when they delivered to Dutch Harbor, Akutan or Port Moller, which often took days because processors couldn't keep up with the fleet. Some boats even steamed back to Kodiak to deliver because the money was better and the wait was too long at other ports.

SMALL-BOAT CRAB FISHERIES

Dungeness is the smallest of Alaska's major crab species. (Art Sutch)

The king crab fishery of the Bering Sea may be the most widely known of Alaska crab fisheries, but two less majestic crustaceans have provided steady work for small boat fishermen all along the state's coast.

If you find crab for sale on an Alaska dock, it's likely the Dungeness, named for a town in Washington state where the fishery began more than 100 years ago. *Cancer magister* are caught all along the Pacific coast, and in some years the harvest from California, Oregon and Washington swamps that of Alaska. At its peak, the state produced about 10 million pounds a year, mostly from Kodiak and Southeast.

Dungeness are dainty compared to king crab, short-legged, with shells measuring about 6 inches across before they are big enough to harvest and weighing just more than a pound. They live in shallower water than king crab, and can be caught in smaller, round pots by smaller boats. Most fishing is done in the summer, and while king and tanner crab are often exported to larger, more lucrative markets, Dungeness fishermen occasion-ally sell their catch directly off their boats in coastal Alaska towns.

The other crab targeted by small-boat fishermen is the larger of the two tanner crab, *Chionocetes bairdi*. Though tanner crab are also harvested in great numbers in the Bering Sea, fleets from Kodiak, the Alaska Peninsula, Cook Inlet and Prince William Sound target them every winter they can. Unfortunately, many of the tanner crab populations have declined substantially since the mid-1980s.

Tanner crab only became popular with fishermen when king crab stocks began to fall in the 1960s and 1970s, and reached a peak in popularity in the late 1970s. Fishing fell off for unknown reasons, but probably from a combination of warmer water temperatures, increased predation and commercial fishing pressure. Tanner crabbing continues in Kodiak, but at a far lower level than before, and is closed in Cook Inlet and Prince William Sound until stocks improve. ◄

At its peak in 1980, a fleet of 236 boats landed 130 million pounds. It took them less than six weeks, yet the average boat landed $500,000 worth of king crab. A typical deckhand's share was probably $10,000 per week, and many earned far more.

Yet the fishery died even faster than it had grown. The following year, every-one was stunned, including biologists, as fishermen kept pulling nearly empty pots. They finished the season with just 34 million pounds. The 1982 harvest fell to 3 million. The area closed in 1983 and though it reopened in 1984, catches since then have rarely exceeded 15 million pounds.

No one knows why the Bristol Bay fishery crashed so hard, though most believe it was a combination of factors. It now appears that the stock had built to record high levels and that a decline was inevitable, though overfishing may have exacerbated the collapse. The stock has not recovered to even half its former size, and some cite the Magnuson-Stevens Act as a possible cause — as foreign groundfish catches declined throughout the North Pacific, pollock and cod stocks increased and both are known predators of juvenile crab.

Another potential agent was an increase in water temperatures throughout the North Pacific around 1977. Biologists believe the warmer water has helped boost Alaska salmon runs to record levels and fear the opposite may be true for crustaceans.

Though Kodiak came to its prominence as one of Alaska's premier fishing ports because of king crab, it also was the center of a thriving shrimp fishery throughout the 1960s and 1970s. But for reasons yet unknown, stocks of trawl- and pot-caught shrimp — all of the genus *Pandalus* — collapsed in Kodiak and Cook Inlet in the early 1980s and have never recovered.

Kachemak Bay and the Alaska Peninsula also lost shrimp and king crab fisheries in the same period.

Whatever affliction caused the declines — overfishing, disease, predation, environment — seems to have affected Alaska shellfish stocks randomly. Kodiak and Southeast fishermen still catch Dungeness crab, but the commercial fishery has been closed for more than a decade in Cook Inlet. Snow crab catches declined but bounced back in Kodiak, and Southeast still has a viable king crab fishery.

BOTTOM LEFT: *Shrimp fishing has declined substantially in recent years. Kodiak and Cook Inlet, which formerly had thriving industries, now see little action. Only in Southeast and Prince William Sound is shrimping a viable commercial enterprise. This 1983 photo shows Fernando Trovao and Neil Mannix bringing a load of shrimp into Homer. (Chlaus Lotscher)*

BELOW: *Deck crew member Chad Wellham lands a pot of* opilio *tanner crab on the* Northern Enterprise *catcher-processor. (Daryl Binney)*

FACING PAGE: *At least 24 hours before a crab opener begins, the fleet gathers for inspection by ADF&G officials. When a boat passes inspection, its registration receives a sticker and the boat is free to leave the dock. This photo, taken from Mt. Ballyhoo (1,589 feet) on Amaknak Island, shows the fleet heading out of Dutch Harbor for crabbing grounds in the Bering Sea. (Dan Parrett)*

ABOVE: *Opilio tanner crab are loaded through a side wall at a shore-based processor at Kodiak. (Harry M. Walker)*

RIGHT: *Opilio tanner crab are being brought ashore at Kodiak. (Harry M. Walker)*

SHELLFISH MARICULTURE

Despite the cloudy skies and cool temperatures, an Alaska farmer breaks into a sweat as he bends over his crop and tears at the weeds. Like farm hands around the world he has no dearth of work, from repairing storm damage and thinning out seedlings to filling out reports and marketing plans.

He's not working a Palmer potato field or carrots on the Kenai, but rather an oyster farm in Kachemak Bay, one of many that constitute the new and rapidly growing shellfish mariculture industry in Alaska. About 50 operations raise oysters, blue mussels and little-neck clams in seaside farms in lower Cook Inlet, Prince William Sound, Southeast and Kodiak.

It's not easy, they all say, and the regulations are taxing, but their work is finally paying off. Consumers rave about the flavor of shellfish grown in the cold, clean waters of Alaska, and markets in Anchorage cannot get enough. The industry has its sights set higher, however — the rest of the U.S. and Japan — and they see a market niche that will only expand as water quality declines elsewhere in the world. The pristine waters of Alaska, they believe, are both the medium and the message.

Oysters are the focus of most attention, and have been since 1910 when the first Alaska shellfish farmers seeded beaches with the Pacific oyster, *Crassostrea gigas*, producing a few bushels a year for 50 years. Even as oyster farms ballooned in Puget Sound, the Gulf of Mexico and elsewhere in succeeding years, Alaska's restrictive policies on everything from leasing state tidelands to importing spat (juvenile oysters) kept all but a few hardy pioneers at bay.

The so-called "blue revolution" of seafood farming hit Alaska in 1988 when the Legislature streamlined the permitting process. Although lawmakers refused to allow salmon farming, shellfish farmers got the green light and almost overnight the number of farms jumped from a handful to more than 70.

Some prospective farmers let their permits lapse after discovering that shellfish mariculture is much like dirt farming, hard work and high investment followed by years of waiting, then more hard work. But those who stuck with it are beginning to reap the rewards. In 1996 some 45 farms reported nearly $5 million in sales and in-water inventory.

Though Alaska's water is largely responsible for the high quality of oysters raised here, it's too cold for bivalves to reproduce in, forcing farmers to buy seedlings from the Lower 48. To achieve their own version of vertical integration, Alaska farmers successfully lobbied for a new shellfish hatchery in Seward. It is expected to provide enough oyster spat for most farms in the state, at lower cost and higher quality than in the past. In conjunction with a nursery in Kachemak Bay where the seedlings are quadrupled in size, the improved seed stock should boost farmers' yields and reduce growing time dramatically.

Alaska's shellfish mariculture industry will never approach the production of farms Outside because of restrictions on how much of the state-owned coastline will be leased. But farmers look to the day when fresh, farm-raised shellfish from Alaska is served year-round in the finest white-tablecloth restaurants of the world. ◄

Six acres of blue buoys mark a network of sunken lines at the first experimental oyster farm in Halibut Cove off Kachemak Bay in lower Cook Inlet. (Janet R. Klein)

Though the smaller shellfish fisheries around Alaska keep a few boats busy, the industry was devastated when Bristol Bay king crab collapsed in the early 1980s. Many boats were converted into trawlers and returned to the Bering Sea for pollock and cod. The remaining crabbers focused on smaller amounts of brown and blue king crab, and on a pair of species they had previously slighted.

The spindly legged *Chionoecetes bairdi* and *C. opilio*, better known to consumers as snow crab, are featured in all-you-can-eat seafood restaurants across the United States. Both had been fished during the 1970s, but as king crab supplies dried up in 1980s, the demand for lower-cost alternatives made snow crab a natural substitute. Prices rose, stocks were healthy, and another boom was on, albeit slower and less valuable than the glorious king crab.

Since the big bust in 1980, the Bering Sea crab fisheries have maintained a relatively steady pace. Though the king crab seasons often are less than a week long, there are several from August through November, and the *opilio* fishery provides several months of winter work. All are monitored more closely than before, with lower quotas and strict bycatch limits on the other crab species. The bycatch by bottom trawlers has also been reduced, with some areas of the Bering Sea closed to bottom trawling

ABOVE: *Spindly legged tanner crab are among several species of crustaceans that provide work for coastal Alaska fishermen. This load is being delivered to a processor in Petersburg. In 1996, fishermen delivering to the Southeast town received $43 million for their total catch of all species. (Don Cornelius)*

RIGHT: *Every crab must be checked to ensure it's of legal size and sex. (Joel Gay)*

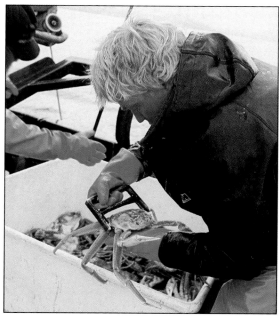

altogether to protect critical habitat, especially for juvenile crab.

The crab are not alone in gaining more protection. Congress in 1988 passed the Commercial Fishing Vessel

Safety Act and for the first time began regulating the fishing industry. Boats must carry a minimum amount of

Even small boats can participate in the crab fisheries, provided the weather is suitable. Here skipper Jack Ranwiler delivers tanner crab from Kachemak Bay to Homer. (Chlaus Lotscher)

safety equipment, including life rafts that are inspected annually, emergency locator devices, flares and strobe lights. Monthly safety drills are now mandatory and every vessel must have at least one person on board with first aid training.

Though the North Pacific fishing industry is still among the most

dangerous in the United States, the number of vessel sinkings fell dramatically in the early 1990s and the death toll dropped by half. The tremendous risks remain and boats still disappear, but skippers and crew are far more likely to see their homes again now than during the lucrative, golden days of king crab fishing. ◄

DIVE FISHERIES

One of the newest fisheries in Alaska doesn't involve hooks, lines or nets of any form. From Southeast to Kodiak and the Alaska Peninsula, divers slip underwater to pluck their harvest off the sea floor — spiny sea urchins, fat sea cucumbers, abalone and a type of clam called the geoduck.

The first dive fishing began in the early 1970s when a handful of divers targeted the pinto or northern abalone, *Haliotis kamschatkana*, in Southeast waters. As long as prices were low — around $1 a pound — there was little interest in the fishery. But as prices eventually doubled and then doubled again, interest boomed. Catches jumped from 6,000 pounds a year to as much as 370,000 in 1981. The abalone could not keep pace, however, and harvests have gradually dwindled until, in 1996, the fishery was closed altogether.

As divers began to explore underwater fishing areas in the late 1970s, they also found a clam known to biologists as *Panopea abrupta*. The popular name is spelled "geoduck," but pronounced "gooey-duck." Because it is known to be a slow-growing, long-lived shellfish susceptible to accumulating toxins in parts of its body, ADF&G took a more conservative approach to developing the fishery. Since fishing began in 1985, harvests have held steady at around 200,000 pounds a year worth roughly $2 a pound.

One of the ugliest animals underwater is the giant red sea cucumber, which looks like a short piece of old, thick rope but has a delicious flavor, according to its fans. The harvest of *Parastichopus californicus* didn't begin until the mid-1980s, and has hovered around 1 million pounds a year throughout the 1990s, bringing dive fishermen $1 million or more in a season.

Sea urchins are valued for their gonads, which are considered a delicacy in Japan, and Alaska divers have been happy to search the sea floor for two varieties, the red (*Strongylocentrotus fanciscanus*) and the green (*S. drobachiensis*). Wearing SCUBA tanks or a breathing tube attached to a dive boat called hookah gear, they slowly comb the depths and put their prickly catch into mesh bags before returning to the surface. Most of the fishing effort is in Southeast, where upwards of 3 million pounds have been caught in a year.

Budget cuts have forced ADF&G to take a go-slow approach on urchins, too, which spurred the agency, local processors and some Southeast municipalities to agree on a unique approach to management. Using private and public funds, the fishing industry put up the money required to study urchin grounds and develop a management plan. After seeing the results of more than a year of test fishing throughout the region, the Board of Fisheries approved the new program for startup in 1997. Proponents believe sea urchin fishing could bring several million dollars a year into the Southeast economy.

The fishery has an uncertain future, however, because of sea otters. The cute marine mammals have a voracious appetite for urchins, and have wiped out urchin beds in several areas. If otter populations continue to boom in Southeast, dive fishermen may have to look elsewhere for income. ◄

Sea urchins are plucked off the sea bottom by divers in one of the newest fisheries in Alaska. The interior of a red sea urchin contains five sections, each with a gonad, which are the part of the animal used for food. (Charlie Ess)

OBSERVING:
THE FUTURE OF OUR SEAS

BY DARYL BINNEY

I had a friend named Brian who was a fisherman. He always dreaded going back to sea. Yet once out at sea, it seemed as though he never wanted to leave. I never could understand his behavior, until I had been an observer for several years. Then, to my surprise, I found myself in Brian's shoes.

Choosing to become an observer had been a difficult decision. In the past my education and work experience had been in forestry and the study of plant communities. I had no prior experience working on boats and little knowledge about fish.

I have always liked new adventures. In the past I had accomplished two life-long goals: being a Peace Corps volunteer in West Africa and hiking the 2,100-mile Appalachian Trail. Similar to becoming a Peace Corps volunteer or hiking the trail, becoming an observer

was like taking on a whole new identity and exploring another aspect of myself at a deeper level. Like these other experiences, I did not have a clue about the world I was entering. I was not fond of oceans and the thought of touching fish was offensive and frightening. I was entering uncharted waters both literally and figuratively.

To become an observer I had to attend and successfully complete an intensive two-and-a-half-week training program conducted by the National Marine Fisheries Service (NMFS) at the National Oceanic and Atmospheric Administration (NOAA) in Seattle. The training included instruction in sampling duties and methods, species identification, fishery regulation, life at sea, and cold water survival and safety. There were many hours of classes, long nights studying and completing assignments that often required much punching of calculators and statistical

computation, and memorization of fish and crab species I had never encountered.

My class consisted of approximately 40 people, the majority young males. They had recently graduated from college with a degree in biology or natural resource management. There were also a large number of former Peace Corps volunteers. Completion of a volunteer service showed you had the tenacity to survive "uncharted waters."

In class we learned about the history of the observer program. The two main programs today are the domestic groundfish observer program and the shellfish observer program.

FACING PAGE: *Crab boats stacked with crab pots are tied up to the dock at Trident's processing plant at Akutan in the Aleutians waiting for the start of the* bairdi *tanner crab season. (Daryl Binney)*

Each is uniquely tailored to meet specific state, regional or federal resource management needs. Despite their differences, each program has the common purpose of collecting unbiased data to monitor commercial harvests, document elements of the catch such as species composition and the bycatch (any species that is not processed) of non-targeted species, and for management of the future resource.

GROUNDFISH OBSERVER PROGRAM

Groundfish observer programs have existed since 1973, but until 1986 American observers only worked on foreign fishing vessels. That year,

observers were placed on domestic vessels fishing in an area of the Bering Sea north of Port Moller in which the North Pacific Fishery Management Council (NPFMC) and the National Marine Fisheries Service (NMFS) had concerns about the bycatch of red king crab. Through early 1989 there were a number of mandatory and voluntary observer programs funded through various means. The level of observer sampling and coverage provided by these programs was low and scattered throughout the groundfish fisheries.

The current domestic groundfish observer program took affect in 1990 for the trawl, longline and pot fisheries in the Bering Sea and Gulf of Alaska. It is managed by the NPFMC and is mandated by the Fishery Conservation and Management Act of 1990. The NMFS provides operational oversight of the program, certification training, definition of observer sampling duties and methods, debriefing of observers and management of the data. The costs associated with managing the program are borne by the federal government, while vessel and processing plant owners pay for the cost of the observers.

The groundfish observer program requires that vessels 125 feet or longer must always carry a NMFS-certified observer. Vessels 60 to 124 feet in length must carry a NMFS-certified observer 30 percent of their fishing days in each calendar quarter of the year in which they fish more than 10 days. Processing plants, both shoreside and floating, are also required to have an observer. Plants processing 1,000 or more metric tons in a month must have an observer in the plant each day they process groundfish, while those processing 500 to 1,000 metric tons must have observers 30 percent of the days they process groundfish. Vessel and plant owners and operators obtain observers from one of the observer contractors certified by NMFS. They pay the contractors directly for the cost of the observers.

FIRST ASSIGNMENT

Upon completion of training, I was assigned to observe on the *Pacific Enterprise*, a 150-foot factory trawler owned by Arctic Alaska with a crew of approximately 30 men. The flight to Dutch Harbor began the start of the actual adventure. I had been given two light-blue baskets to use for sampling. In transit they were used to carry the equipment and forms issued by NMFS. While these baskets were blue, I quickly realized they were a red alert to the fishermen that I was an observer and not one of them. Some diehard fishermen viewed observers as spies, the enemy, etc.

Upon boarding the *Pacific Enterprise*, I met the observer I was to replace. She, too, was an ex-Peace Corps volunteer. It had been her first contract and though definitely excited to depart the vessel, she advised me she had been treated well. She showed me around the *Pacific Enterprise*, the area in the factory where she sampled, and her living quarters. Because I was the only female on board and there was an extra bunk, I was given a 2-person room to myself.

The first few days I was on board the vessel, we were docked at the dock in Dutch Harbor waiting for the engine to be repaired. This was to my advantage as it gave me some time to meet the crew and become familiar with the boat and Dutch Harbor. At night a large percentage of the crew would go to the bars in town and each night I could hear the mate making sure everyone was back on board safely and occasionally monitoring altercations.

One afternoon we were scheduled to leave for the fishing grounds. I took a Dramamine™ tablet for seasickness since I did not know how I would fare once the vessel began moving. We ended up not leaving, the Dramamine™ knocked me out, and I decided to just grin and bear it when we finally did leave.

My first day at sea I felt physically ill and I thought the best thing might be to work. When the first tow, a net full of fish, was hauled in, I went into the factory, the area in the boat containing equipment to process the fish, to sample. As the fish came onto the bleeding or sorting belt, I took random samples and threw these into a large white plastic tote the crew had put there for observers to use. Next I had to sort the sample by species, count the number of fish per species, and get a weight per species. With this data I could later calculate the average weight of each species and what percentage of the catch each species comprised.

Besides being seasick, I was also having to confront my fear of handling fish. To make matters worse, a large portion of my sample consisted of rattails or Grenadiers. They are a big, ugly fish with no commercial value. Being slimy, they are also hard to pick up. The only way to do it is to wrap the tail around your hand. I looked at those fish a long time before I could begin weighing them.

I worked continually that first day to survive the horrid way I was feeling. A day later it felt like I was joining the

Crab bait sits in a tote. The orange mesh bags are full of pieces of chopped herring and the white plastic bait jars contain ground-up herring. A cod is also attached to the bait set-up when available. (Daryl Binney)

human race again, as my body began to adjust to life at sea.

This first time out as an observer was a whirlwind of activity and learning. I averaged 16 hours of work a day and life never stopped long enough to get caught up. We processed rockfish, a spiny fish that requires caution when handling. I remember one night when I went to sleep we were processing rockfish. When I woke, I found out that that season had closed and we were now processing turbot. A turbot's skin resembles the rainbow patterns found in oil slicks; however it

required extra caution when handling because of its sharp teeth.

I learned one major lesson about life at sea on this first trip. Every day was different: Like the day when at one moment we were fishing, and the next moment we had engine problems and headed into port. Operations instantaneously changed from processing fish to getting ready for offload.

I had to understand the fishing operations, adjust to living conditions, and learn the proper protocol. I also had to learn to perform my job. I was kept busy learning the different species,

determining the best method of sampling in terms of time, safety and quality, and becoming familiar with all the paperwork requirements. It was a definite physical, mental and emotional challenge to be on a boat.

When you board a boat, the attitude and actions of the crew can make a significant difference in your adjustment. This is especially true the first time out, when you are learning the ins and outs of boat life. In the early 1990s many of the fishermen had a hard time adjusting to observers being on the boat. This was especially

true for female observers, as many fishermen were either superstitious about women living on boats or they just didn't believe they belonged on a boat. The night foreman did not believe I should be on the *Pacific Enterprise* and one of the deck crew sided with him.

On the other hand, I met a few people who made my life at sea quite enjoyable. It was on the *Pacific Enterprise* that I met my friend Brian. Brian took me under his wing and taught me how to be a good shipmate. The first requirement was that you work hard putting out 110 percent and that you maintain a good attitude. The second requirement was that you pitch in and help out whenever necessary.

In my contract the NMFS mandated that I should not have emotional or physical interaction with the rest of the crew. It was a confusing concept, because I did not know how I could live on a 150-foot boat with 30 other people for more than 60 days and not develop emotional contact.

That was one of the hardest aspects of my job. I struggled between the opposing view of management and the fishing industry. I resolved

Many of the observer assignments begin at Dutch Harbor where the crab fleet readies its vessels for the rough waters of the Bering Sea. (Dan Parrett)

Fishing vessels sometimes tie up at the Spit Dock at Dutch Harbor between seasons or when preparations are underway to head to the fishing grounds. (Dan Parrett)

that rules, regulations and fines are necessary, but I did not agree with all the policy of management nor did I feel that the policies justly recognized the expertise, knowledge and concerns of the fishermen.

There were other aspects of the job that reminded me I was an outsider. The other people on board had a common goal of filling the boat with processed fish. They were a team, with all the different positions (whether it be skipper, engineer, deck crew, factory worker or cook) necessary to produce the finished product. I would have liked to be part of that energy, but instead I was viewed as an outsider. To compensate, I helped bleed or sort the fish when possible.

Being an observer on the *Pacific Enterprise* did have certain advantages over being a crew member. For all practical purposes, I was my own boss. I knew what my daily job requirements were, and it was up to me to make sure they were done in a timely and accurate manner. I had to follow the orders of the skipper, my data went to NMFS and my contractor handled the logistics; but in essence I was on my own.

During this contract NMFS gave me the responsibility to determine which tows I would sample and how many to best represent the overall fishing operation. Since fishing occurred around the clock, it was not possible to sample every tow. Fewer tows were hauled in at night, because the fishing was slower and the tows lasted for a longer duration. To accurately represent this, I sampled more daytime tows. My daily schedule varied, unlike the fishermen who worked a certain shift of 16 hours with eight hours of down time.

The other difference was in pay. Once the boat left port, I was paid a certain rate whether we fished or not.

Most of the crew, however, was paid a percentage of the catch. They were more inspired to work hard every day, as their daily wage was determined by the amount of fish they processed that day. They were more interested in making money while I was more interested in preserving the resource.

The biological duties of an observer, while complex and difficult, were not as emotional. One task was to estimate the weight of as many tows as possible. There were several different ways to determine this. I could either estimate the dimension of the cod end on deck

The catcher boat Silver Spray *rides out a Bering Sea storm. Ice buildup can pose a danger for vessels and crews sometimes spend hours chipping ice from their boat. (Daryl Binney)*

or estimate the area of the holding tank filled with fish, and it was up to me to choose the most precise method. Another duty was to sample a certain number of tows to determine species composition, average weight of each species, and bycatch or composition of unprocessed fish. There were also several different methods to choose from to best sample the tow. My sampling was done in the factory near the sorting area and the data was later transcribed onto various forms.

Naturally, paperwork comprised a large part of my duties. There were many statistical calculations to be done. I was also required to record information about the daily fishing operation such as location, duration of tow, and the skipper's estimate of haul weight, bycatch and production, figures that were gotten from the skipper's logbook. Additionally, I recorded interactions with marine mammals or any violation I saw regarding retention of illegal species, disposal of garbage at sea, etc. The last requirement was to keep a logbook for the Alaska Department of Fish and Game in which I recorded my daily work activities and the fishing operation.

Occasionally, observers were also given special projects. On the *Pacific Enterprise*, I was assigned to collect the otoliths of a fish species my boat was processing. Otoliths are a piece of cartilage with concentric lines on them, much like the rings of a tree section. These lines tell scientists the age of the fish and information about its yearly growth rate. I chose to collect otoliths of the shortspine thornyhead rockfish species as it was an opalescent red color and quite beautiful. Handling fish was becoming a bit easier.

I can remember having problems figuring out how to recover the otoliths, but my friend Brian showed me how. It was great to have him to talk to on the boat even though at times our jobs opposed each other.

For example, certain tows might contain a lot of bycatch such as crab, salmon or halibut. The bycatch is suppose to be sorted out of the tow before the tow is dumped into the holding tank. This requires sorting on deck and more work for the deck crew, so the tows are usually just dumped into the hold. If it was a real dirty tow (a tow containing a lot of bycatch), the fishermen, including Brian, would try to hide the bycatch from me. In these situations I really had to monitor the fishing operation to accurately sample the tow and the bycatch contained within it. Once again I found myself an outsider, even with Brian.

There are some moments that really stand out in my mind from my time on the *Pacific Enterprise*. My favorite was the day we saw a large pod of killer whales. My skipper called down into the factory where I was working to tell me to come on deck. There were at least 20 whales, and it was a spectacular sight. To see their fins arch through the air and catch a glimpse of their massive bodies made the sea come alive in a new way. For the rest of that day and evening there were always a few riding in the wake of our

A deck crew member hooks up a cable to totes containing opilio *tanner crab. The totes will be dumped into the hopper on board the catcher-processor* Pacific Wind. *Another crew member removes all crab from the pot on the launcher before the pot is stored on deck. (Daryl Binney)*

LEFT: *Pitchers throw opilio tanner crab into a brailer that will be hoisted aboard a processing ship in the Bering Sea. (Daryl Binney)*

ABOVE: *Bundled up, deck boss Bob Pattison runs the hydraulics to store the crab pots on the deck of the catcher-processor Olympic during the 1995 opilio tanner crab season. (Daryl Binney)*

FACING PAGE: *Deck crew members of the catcher-processor Alaskan Enterprise hoist a pot filled with herring bait transferred from another vessel during a fall crab season. (Daryl Binney)*

boat. There were many, many more memories but this remains my favorite.

As the boat became full of product, the energy of the boat intensified. Once the freezers were full the boat would go to port to offload. The final signal it was time to go in was when any supplies stored in the freezer were moved into empty bunk space or on one of two tables in the galley. The living space became quite crowded, but everyone was too happy to care. After a month at sea, it would be great to be on land again.

Even my departure from the vessel was an adventure. The mate and I were the only crew members leaving. We were to be dropped off to the Arctic Alaska processor and were to catch a flight back to Dutch the next day. It was midnight when we departed the *Pacific Enterprise*, a storm was raging and we had to get craned off the boat onto the processor. The storm continued, no planes flew for two days and we caught a ride in on a catcher boat that was being towed to Dutch by another boat. It was a long, slow, rocky trip and it reinforced the most important lesson I had learned at sea, that you never knew what the sea had in store for you.

After departing my vessel, the *Pacific Enterprise*, I had to go through the debriefing process. In debriefing all paperwork is reviewed by a staff member of NMFS in Seattle. All paperwork must be correctly filled out and any statistical errors recalculated to complete the debriefing process. During this period, paperwork requirements were intense, so debriefing could be quite an ordeal and require a week of correcting papers, cleaning and turning in equipment and any specimens that had been collected, and completing a final summary report.

I experienced a bit of culture shock upon leaving Dutch Harbor and hitting

This shark came up in a net of pollock on The Dawn, *a trawler out of Kodiak. (Daryl Binney)*

the mainland. My life had been going about 10 knots per hour; life on land definitely moved more rapidly. Life at sea was so different from being on land.

SECOND SEASON

I had to admit I enjoyed being an observer, and the next summer found me back at sea observing. No longer a novice, I worked on three different kinds of boats. Each type of fishing dictated a unique set of sampling conditions, so my actual job duties and how they were carried out varied depending on the type of vessel I was on.

The first boat I worked on was the 135-foot *SeaDawn* trawler with a crew of five. Bunks were scarce and a padded bench in the wheelhouse became my bunk. The boat was fishing for pollock and usually only two or three tows were hauled in a day. If fishing went well we would be back in port in three days to offload. The work load on this boat was quite easy for an observer, especially compared to the *Pacific Enterprise*, and most of the sampling was done at the processing plant during offload.

The next boat I worked on was the 343-foot *Arctic Storm* factory trawler. I flew up to St. Paul in the Pribilofs to meet the boat and had a day to wait before it showed up. I spent the day exploring St. Paul Island and visiting the sea lion rookery there.

The next day I boarded the *Arctic Storm*. There was a crew of more than

100 that consisted of both males and females. The living quarters on this boat were luxurious in terms of living standards at sea. I shared a room with three other females. Because they were on various shifts and my work was done during all shifts, I had to be non-intrusive during their down-time.

The *Arctic Storm* was fishing for pollock and they often pulled in 200 metric tons of fish in a tow. This boat was much cleaner than the other boats I had worked on, but as a result it lost some of the rustic feel of a fishing boat. As an example, the wheelhouse on this boat reminded me of *Star Wars*. It was large, plush and full of sophisticated equipment. I enjoyed being on this vessel, but I decided that at this point in my career I longed for the boats with the more rugged living and fishing conditions.

I got my wish, and the next boat I boarded was the 69-foot *Masonic* schooner. We did a 13-day trip longlining for black cod with a makeshift crew of six fishermen and myself. One of the crew Jim, an elder fishermen, had fished for many years. It was an honor and privilege to work with him. He was knowledgeable, skilled and had a great attitude. Even though it was a makeshift crew, the whole trip was quite enjoyable and it turned out to be a profitable trip for the fishermen.

Physically the *Masonic* was difficult for me to be on. It was small and I was more prone to feeling seasick. The

Crew members from the processor Coastal Star *are hoisted onto the deck of the catcher boat* Theresa Marie. *These crew members, called pitchers, unload crab from the holding tank of the catcher boat into brailers that are then craned over to the processor and dropped into a big hopper. (Daryl Binney)*

galley was in the bow of the boat and four of the crew's bunks were there as well. Sitting in the bow was usually a rocky ride and I could not stay there for long. As the trip progressed, the stench of herring on dirty gear stored in the bunks in the galley did not make it any easier.

The skipper, Mark, gave me the privilege of sleeping down in the engine room at the stern of the boat, a nice gesture as the ride was much smoother there. I crawled down into this area of the boat and the two bunks that were there had about 2 feet of space above them. The closed-in quarters were dark, but at least the motion of the boat was mellower there, otherwise I am not sure my stomach would have made it.

On the *Masonic* I got to see how a longline fishery with hooks worked. I was also required to use a different sampling strategy to best sample this fishery. Since being on deck was much more comfortable than being in the galley or my bunk, I ended up sampling every string and developed a kinship with the dolphins that would ride the

bow of the boat. One night we were up late pulling in a string and a fur seal appeared right off the side of our boat, lounging on its back. That sure gave our tired crew a burst of energy!

Even though the *Masonic* was physically a difficult boat for me to be on, I felt fortunate to have had the experience. One thing I learned is that the crew and the morale on the boat play a big part in determining the kind of trip it will be. Once again Brian's words rang true. I also left that boat in awe that some fishermen

A deck crew member of the Deep Sea Harvester *catcher-processor undoes the pot tie that holds the door closed as a wave washes across the deck during a* bairdi *tanner crab opening. The buoy and line will be taken out of the pot and the pot baited before it is launched overboard. (Daryl Binney)*

work in those conditions on every trip, knowing they will experience some seasickness every time they return to work until their body adjusts.

Working out at sea I heard about the shellfish observer program from various fishermen such as Brian. Even on a boat word gets around. It was described as higher pay and the work-load was less, so I decided to try it to broaden my background and because I was not overly pleased with some of the changes occurring in the domestic groundfish observer program. My friend Brian had switched over to crabbing as it promised more money and greater adventure, so his decision added to my curiosity.

SHELLFISH OBSERVER PROGRAM

The shellfish observer program was mandated in the fall of 1988 by the Alaska Board of Fisheries. The number of vessels capable of processing crab at sea had increased and outstripped the monitoring ability of the Dutch Harbor ADF&G onshore sampling program. The shellfish observer program was initially directed at vessels processing king crab and *bairdi* tanner crab at sea. Later, the Alaska Board of Fisheries amended the state shellfish regulations to include observer coverage in the *opilio* tanner crab fishery as well. It also gave ADF&G authority to place observers on commercial vessels participating in other Alaska shell fisheries when such action would facilitate the only means to collect biological and fishery management data.

Historically, it wasn't until after World War II when Americans began showing interest in Alaska's crab resources that the Japanese and Soviets were already exploring. As the fishing capacity of the American fleet continued to grow, foreign fishing for king crab was no longer allowed in 1974 and for all other crab by 1980.

Competition among U.S. fishermen resulted in the evolution of larger, faster and more efficient catcher boats. In the early 1980s vessels capable of both catching and processing crab began to appear in greater numbers among the fleet. In 1987 these catcher-processors accounted for 20 percent of the red king crab harvest in the Bering Sea. Because this crab was processed at sea, it was unavailable for examination by ADF&G. Thus the need for an observer program.

The shellfish observer program is similar to the groundfish observer program in many ways. ADF&G provides the operational oversight, certification training, definition of observer sampling duties and methods, debriefing of observers and management of the data. Vessels hire observers directly through third party contractors. The contractors provide all logistical and administrative functions, assign observers to vessels, make travel arrangements, and assure observers receive adequate training before being certified. The data the shellfish observer collects go to ADF&G. Unlike the groundfish program, most of the sampling equipment is provided by the contractor while the observers must supply their own rain gear and boots.

On Christmas day, 1991, I flew to Anchorage to attend a seven-day training course to become a shellfish observer. The training covered everything from crab biology to marine survival. After completing the class, I was flown to Dutch Harbor to take a four-hour certification exam given by the staff of the ADF&G Observer Program. The exam tested my knowledge of fisheries regulations, observer responsibilities, data collection procedures, crab identification, evidence collection and proper radio reporting procedures. A score of 90 or

Assistant factory foreman Roy Glison boxes opilio *tanner crab on the* Northern Enterprise *catcher-processor. (Daryl Binney)*

better was necessary to be given a probationary certification. The observer could then work at sea, but must undergo a 30-day review before full certification would be granted.

FIRST TIME AS A SHELLFISH OBSERVER

I successfully completed my exam. It was mid-January and the start of the 1992 *opilio* tanner crab fishery, when I boarded the *Northern Enterprise* catcher-processor. This was also my first time at sea in the winter. I bunked with the cook, who quickly informed me he didn't believe women belonged on boats. He reminded me of my night

foreman on the *Pacific Enterprise*, only I had to share a room with him.

My biological sampling duties included measuring the size of 100 crab each day. This data would be used to determine the age distribution of the crab being harvested. I also had to count and measure everything that was caught in a pot, doing four pots each day. This information would be used to help estimate crab populations and to predict future trends. Other biological duties included finding average catch weights and recording information about the fishing effort such as location, number of pots fishing, production, etc.

Old Trafford, c. 1910

The Oval, 1905

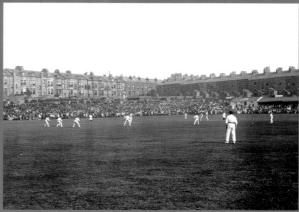

Marine Parade, Scarborough, 1913

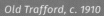

Sydney Cricket Ground, 1983

Northlands Road, Southampton, 1974

Tilford, Surrey, 1971

Trent Bridge, 1973

The WACA, Perth, c. 1905

New Road, Worcester, 1936

1954

ADELAIDE OVAL

Still maintaining a view to Adelaide Cathedral

With the River Torrens to the south and 760 hectares of Adelaide parklands stretching to the north, the much-admired Adelaide Oval was created from twelve acres of ground leased from the Adelaide City Council in 1871. As ovals go, it was rather long and narrow, which pleased batsmen who hooked and cut, but not those who specialised in straight sixes.

The first ever match in 1873 saw a British-born team take on a side of Colonial players, followed the next year by a visit from W.G. Grace's XI. After beating Yorke's Bay XXII, Grace's team won their game against a South Australia XXII. A half-holiday was declared for

ABOVE: Queen Elizabeth II meets two local South Australian teams at the Adelaide Oval on 19th March 1954. The Queen's eight-week visit was her first, indeed, it was the first visit to Australia by any British ruling monarch.

the occasion and a fine crowd of 5,000 attended. In the 1880s the Adelaide Oval took its place as a major sporting venue. The ground hosted its first Test – only the sixth to have taken place – in 1884, staged a football match played under electric light which attracted a crowd of 8,000, and also hosted its first Grand Final in Aussie rules football.

One of the outstanding cricket players of this or any era was the South Australian player George Giffen. In 1891, he recorded one of the great performances in first-class cricket against Victoria, scoring 271 runs and taking 16 wickets for 166 in the match. He was the first person to achieve the double of 1000 runs and 100 wickets, all against England. His career figures

of 10,000 runs and 1,000 wickets have never been surpassed by any Australian.

Development of the ground was slow. A wooden members' stand, built in 1882, lasted for 10 years until replaced by the George Giffen grandstand which survived until 2009. Separate Ladies and Smokers stands were constructed in 1895 on the northern side of the Members' Stand. Majestic Moreton Bay fig trees were planted in the 1890s which gave shade to spectators and blocked free views of the cricket by non-paying passers-by. At the same time, earth from the banks of the River Torrens was used to construct a mound which became the Adelaide Hill. When the famous hand-operated scoreboard was installed there

in 1911, the Hill became an institution and a home for the noisiest elements of the crowd.

Cricket at the Adelaide Oval has not been short of drama. Probably the defining moment of the 1932/33 Ashes 'Bodyline' series occurred when England's fast bowler Harold Larwood struck and injured the Australian batsmen Bill Woodfull and Bert Oldfield. In 1992, the West Indies won the fourth Test by one run when the Australian number 11, Craig McDermott, edged Courtney Walsh to the wicket-keeper, and in

ABOVE: Unlike many of the Australian mega stadia, the Adelaide Oval has maintained views to the parkland and cathedral beyond.

2010

1999, the Sri Lankan team almost abandoned the game when Muttiah Muralitharan was continually no-balled for throwing in an ODI against England.

Domestically, by 1934 South Australia had gone almost ten years without winning the Sheffield Shield. With Bradman dissatisfied at New South Wales, the state wooed him with a business offer and immediately reaped the benefit, winning the Sheffield Shield twice in the next four years. Beginning with three centuries in his first three games, Bradman made 18 centuries and only one duck in his new career, which ended in 1948.

Ground development never stood still in these years with the construction of the Sir Donald Bradman stand in 1990 and the Chappell Stands in 2003. But pressure was building for a new Aussie rules venue.

Faced with the enormous cost of a new stadium, the government preferred to re-purpose the Adelaide Oval, as long as the Heritage Status features were preserved. Particularly important were the Northern Mound, the

ABOVE: Looking across the Oval and the River Torrens towards the central business district of Adelaide.

scoreboard, the fig trees and the view beyond the stadium. Not everyone was happy. The Kaurna, the original people of the Adelaide Plains, still have unrecognised territorial claims.

So the Adelaide Oval is now officially a multi-sport stadium. This meant demolishing the Giffen, Bradman and Chappell stands and building a monster new West Stand. The ground capacity has been increased from 34,000 to about 50,000, depending on the sport. Test matches since 2013 have been played on drop-in pitches, spelling the end for what was reckoned to be the best batting wicket in Australia. Amid the turmoil, the 1911 scoreboard and the fig trees survived.

ABOVE: With the change of dimensions in 2014 to 183m x 134m for the benefit of Aussie rules football, one sad casualty is the all-run five, which was possible before.

c. 1995

c. 1995

AGEAS BOWL

The new home of Hampshire cricket became an invaluable Test venue

LEFT: In 1987, Mark Nicholas, captain of Hampshire, and club vice-Chairman Bill Hughes, went out for an Italian meal. Nicholas was concerned about Hampshire's future at the County Ground in Southampton. Northlands Road – the County's home since 1885 – was surrounded by residential buildings with little room for expansion. Of the main outgrounds, development at Bournemouth didn't really make sense in terms of cost, and Portsmouth only hosted two games a year. Supposing, Nicholas mused, that Hampshire could centralise its cricketing activities and build a modern stadium in the Southampton area? It was an idea which received general support in the club, but it was well into the 1990s before Hampshire found what they were looking for – a 150-acre site owned by Queen's College, Oxford, at West End, just north of the M27. An architect was selected – Sir Michael Hopkins, designer of the Mound Stand at Lord's. Mark Nicholas, former England batsman Robin Smith and off-spinner Sean Udal stood in the empty field and toasted the future home of Hampshire cricket in champagne.

LEFT: The greenfield site of what would become the Rose Bowl, with the M27 motorway nearby.

ABOVE: There probably wouldn't be a Hampshire club today without Rod Bransgrove. After construction began in 1997, costs spiralled out of control and the club became technically insolvent. Rod Bransgrove, with a fortune made in pharmaceuticals and a passionate interest in cricket, agreed to become Chairman. He bankrolled the club, although the figures were eye-watering – an operating loss of over £1 million in 2002 and an overall loss of more than £4 million. Further large sums were required in 2011 and 2012.

Today, the Rose Bowl (or the Ageas Bowl as it is known for sponsorship reasons) has found ways to balance the books. A four-star 175-room Hilton hotel built in 2015 with suites named after Hampshire cricketers, the 18-hole Boundary Lakes golf course opened in 2017, and pop concerts, all contribute to financial stability. The hotel is integrated into the ground and this feature was ideal during the Covid pandemic, making it a bio-secure base – along with Old Trafford – for the West Indies and Pakistan Tests

in 2020. Whether this will earn Rod Bransgrove any Brownie points in his attempt to achieve perhaps his greatest ambition remains to be seen. The Ageas Bowl has hosted a small number of Test matches but, despite its magnificent facilities, not yet an Ashes Test. Even hosting the final of the World Test Championship in 2021, though a nice consolation prize, was not quite the same thing.

LEFT: It must be galling that a lovely ground with well over a hundred years of history is remembered mainly for a single game. But the story of the match between Derbyshire and Lancashire at Buxton in June 1975 is well worth retelling. Saturday, the first day of the three-day game, was blazing hot and Lancashire made 477 for 5 declared. After the Sunday rest day, the teams turned up on Monday when, out of nowhere, thick snow began to fall on Britain's highest county ground. Play was abandoned immediately. Dickie Bird, the umpire, didn't need long to come to the decision: 'The snow was level with the top of my boots!' On Tuesday, to Derbyshire's surprise, play began on time. The pitch had now become a batter's nightmare. A Derbyshire player, Ashley Harvey-Walker, took out his false teeth and handed them to Dickie Bird, saying he would be back for them soon. 'He collected his teeth three balls later!' Bird recalled. Derby were bowled out for 42 and 87 and lost by the enormous margin of an innings and 348 runs. The game was finished by 3.20pm. Still, 42 wasn't the lowest team score at Buxton. That was 36 in 1954 – by Lancashire!

BELOW: A beautiful place to watch cricket with vistas to the distant Peak District National Park.

ABOVE: Derbyshire continued to play occasional games at Buxton, usually against Lancashire. But outgrounds in general were at a disadvantage in preparing pitches to county standard and in 1986 the pitch was considered unsatisfactory and the ground dropped from the rota of Derbyshire grounds. Buxton had hosted a total of 44 County Championship matches and ten limited overs games.

The home club, Buxton Cricket Club (1853), has a rich and varied history, not least, as it admits, in the number of leagues in which it has played. By the turn of the century, with 'aging players, little investment and few volunteers', the club was faltering. Under new management, the last ten years have seen consistent progress on and off the field. In 2016 the club returned to its county roots in the Derbyshire County League and 2021 has seen continued revival with a fourth XI joining its three senior men's teams and the opening of a women's section. And, though it has been known to snow during practice matches in April, there has been no recurrence of the events of 2nd June 1975.

ST LAWRENCE GROUND, CANTERBURY
Little changed since its heyday in the 1970s

1970

LEFT: At one time in the 1840s and 50s, both Beverley CC and Maidstone CC called themselves Kent Cricket Club. Eventually, the clubs merged in 1870 to form Kent County Cricket Club. The new club was based at the St Lawrence Ground, whose first groundsman in the 1840s was a famous name, Fuller Pilch. It was here that W.G. Grace scored the first triple century in first-class cricket in 1876 after his side, the MCC, had followed on. A famous curiosity was the lime tree which stood inside the boundary line. This photograph, by Patrick Eager, shows it outside the field of play for a May 1970 Gillette Cup match between Kent and Worcestershire. Following a dispute, it was decided that if a ball hit the tree it would count as four and a batsman caught out from a rebound off the tree would not be out. Three batsmen actually cleared the tree with enormous hits – the West Indies' Learie Constantine, Middlesex's Jim Smith and the little-known amateur Arthur Watson of Sussex.

BELOW: The 1970s were a prime period for Kent. The county won ten trophies under Colin Cowdrey and Mike Denness, including County Championships in 1970 and 1978, a shared Championship in 1977 and a host of one-day trophies. In 1999, the iconic lime tree was diagnosed with fungus. Expected to survive for another 10 years, high winds snapped it in two in January 2005 and the club's pre-eminent landmark was gone. Carl Hooper in 1992 was the fourth and last batsman to clear its massive branches. The club had planned a replacement tree but, as it was still only a sapling when it was called in to bat, it was planted outside the boundary ropes but within the playing area. The club has drawn up many development plans for the The Spitfire Ground, St Lawrence (as it is known commercially) in the 2000s, but most of them failed to come to fruition. One idea which did make the cut was a 'Legends Walkway'. The players – chosen by the public – included Alfred Mynn, Godfrey Evans, Doug Wright, Alan Knott and Derek Underwood.

c. 1910

NEWLANDS CRICKET GROUND, CAPE TOWN

One of cricket's most spectacular backdrops – Table Mountain

ABOVE: The creation of Newlands Cricket Ground goes back to the mid-1880s when the Western Province Cricket Club of Wynberg took out a 25-year lease for £100 on a nearby piece of farmland in the shadow of spectacular Table Mountain. Each life member of the club was expected to donate £25 towards the cost of acquiring the ground, and £350 was raised for the cost of a suitable pavilion. The first match took place between Home Born, for which read the English, and Colonial Born, meaning the locals, who ran out the winners. Only five years after Test cricket was played at Lord's, Newlands hosted its first Test match in 1889 between South Africa and England. South Africa lost by an innings and generally did not have a good record at the ground, winning only twice in thirty years. In 1902 attendance records were broken as 10,000 cricket fans crowded into the ground to watch the first visit of the Australians. The ground was called 'a cricketing paradise' and attracted much praise from visiting English cricketers such as Sir Pelham Warner and C. Aubrey Smith, who would go on to form a cricket club in Hollywood.

ABOVE: Between 1991 and 1997 numerous changes were made to the ground to increase its income-generating potential. Large portions of the grass embankments were replaced by pavilions, increasing the capacity to 25,000. As Newlands is used for cricket only 35 days a year, to generate extra income the stadium rights have been sold to Six Gun Grill. A major commercial redevelopment of the precinct started in October 2020. In recent years, Newlands has become something of a home banker for South Africa or, as the *Daily Mail* said, 'Don't be seduced by Newlands: South Africa are almost unbeatable there.' Since 1995, the Proteas have won 23 of 32 games at the ground and lost only four. (Although one of those was to England in 2020.) With teams containing Hashim Amla, Allan Donald, Jacques Kallis, A.B. de Villiers, Kagisio Rabada and Dale Steyn, to name only a few of the players who have played since 2000, it is easy to see why.

c. 1920

CENTRAL GROUND, HASTINGS
Once home to a celebrated end-of-season cricket festival

ABOVE: Looking across the ground towards South Terrace, around 1920. The Hastings Unitarian Church (1868), with its three distinctive arched windows, is just down the road from the Quaker Meeting House, located behind the sight screen.

1898

When the Hastings Festival was in its pomp, it hosted the great names of cricket. W.G. Grace played here over forty times, Ranjitsinhji scored the first double hundred at the ground and, in 1925, Jack Hobbs scored his 16th century of the year. This remained the most first-class centuries ever scored in a season until Denis Compton scored his 17th century in 1947 – also at Hastings. Bradman played here for the 1948 Australians and scored his obligatory hundred.

The Central Recreation Ground, as it was known, hosted 228 first-class matches as well as 14 one-day games. The Hastings Festival, which took place at the season's end in September, changed over the years. Prior to World War I, composite XIs played, such as South vs North, Gentleman vs Players (seven times) and an England XI vs Australia. There were also unlikely sounding matches such as The Rest vs Lancashire and Yorkshire, which included seven Yorkies, and Capped vs Uncapped in 1923, being the England team against those yet to play for England – won, as sometimes happens, by the pretenders.

Going back in time, it is thought that the part of Hastings where the cricket ground is located was once a natural harbour which gradually silted up. In the 12th century a priory was established, but lasted only a couple of centuries before becoming uninhabitable because of the swampiness of the area. Drawings of the 1700s show the land was nothing but marshes and fields. In the 1830s the stream area was culverted and drained and turned into a cricket ground, which

was originally known as Priory Meadow before the name was changed in 1864. Sussex began to play at Hastings the same year, one of 17 grounds the county has used, some of them not even in Sussex. Cricket did not have exclusive use of the site; a wide range of other entertainments was available, including circuses, archery and football, and, on one occasion, the display of the skeleton of a 70-ton whale which had become beached at Pevensey. Four years later Hastings hosted a game in the first tour by an Australian side – the Australian Indigenous team, a match which was drawn.

Only two championship games were played from 1865 to 1896, although after the World War II, championship cricket became the norm. The ground

was also a busy centre of women's cricket from the 1950s, as well as club matches, schools' cricket and charity games.

But given its location and size, the ground had obvious commercial potential. The Maidstone and District bus company had already leased a corner of the ground by the entrance in the 1930s and in 1959

ABOVE LEFT: W.G. Grace at the 1898 Hastings Festival with William Carless (left), the Secretary of the Festival. The photo is looking towards South Terrace, with the Prince's Hotel, at No. 10, visible over W.G.'s shoulder.

ABOVE: Today, the Unitarian Church and the Quaker Meeting House face the Priory Centre on South Terrace. The Prince's Hotel is now Pissarro's Brasserie.

1981

LEFT: The 'Brumbrella' rain cover is deployed during the 2nd Texaco Trophy One Day International between England and Australia on 6th June 1981.

OPPOSITE: The England cricket team prior to their first Test match against Australia at Edgbaston on 29th May 1902. Left to right, back row: George Hirst, Dick Lilley, Bill Lockwood, Len Braund, Wilfred Rhodes and John Thomas Tyldesley. Front row: C.B. Fry, Frank Stanley Jackson, Archie MacLaren, Kumar Shri Ranjitsinhji and Gregory Jessop.

BELOW: Worcestershire, including Moeen Ali, huddle during the Vitality T20 Blast Final between Worcestershire Rapids and Essex Eagles at Edgbaston on 21st September 2019.

England became the number one-ranked Test team by beating India, Alastair Cook scoring 294. Although that was some way off being the ground's highest individual score: against Durham in 1994, Brian Lara scored 501 not out, the highest-ever score in first-class cricket.

If William Ansell came back today, the ground would no doubt meet with his approval, although his stand was pulled down in the blitz of building work in 2011. A third of the old stadium was demolished and two huge new stands erected, along with the famous E-shaped floodlights. Further redevelopment of the stadium and environs never ceases and Phase 3 is in the pipeline, mainly concerned with the erection of The Residences – the three massive residential tower blocks will be completed in time for the 2022 Commonwealth Games, a women's T20 tournament and the England vs South Africa men's Test match.

If Edgbaston is beginning to sound monumental, the Eric Hollies Stand – named after the leg-spinner who played for Warwickshire for 25 years – does its anarchic best to 'out-Gabba' the Gabba. Its atmosphere has been described as 'electric' and 'brilliant'. That's not bad for a venue that started out as 12 acres of rough grazing.

c. 1962

THE GABBA

Brisbane's cricket ground is about to be flattened...

The Gabba is short for Woolloongabba, a suburb in the east coast city of Brisbane. The name is Aboriginal and may mean 'a fighting place', recalling a big tribal fight which took place nearby in 1853. Alternatively, it may stem from 'wulunkoppa', an Aboriginal word meaning swampy parkland or 'one-mile swamp'. The area certainly needed to be drained before the first game could take place in 1896.

Other grounds existed in the area, principally the Exhibition Ground, which staged Test matches and Queensland's Sheffield Shield matches. When that venue closed in 1931, Test and Shield cricket was transferred to the Gabba. The ground staged its first Test match in 1931 when Australia played South Africa.

Bradman scored 226 in that match, but for once does not hold the record for most centuries on the ground, which belongs to the Australian opening batsman David Warner. As late as the 1940s, seating consisted of three rudimentary wooden grandstands, although shade was provided by some magnificent Moreton Bay fig trees.

The first Test of an Ashes series is usually played at the Gabba in the second week of December. It is the most northerly of the Test venues, and pitch preparation is a few weeks ahead of other grounds. In any event, the other grounds have to be juggled in wherever the programme will allow, once Melbourne and Sydney have claimed Christmas and New Year.

Australia always get off to a good start at the Gabba, where the team has an outstanding record, losing only one Test match since 1988. In the fourth Test of the 2020/21 series, India scored a magnificent 329-7 in the fourth innings to win the series 2-1. Brisbanites would still say they are unbeaten whenever the first Test is played at Brisbane. Certainly, Australian players and coaches prefer to start the series at the Gabba rather than Perth or Adelaide, where they lost in 2016 and 2018.

OPPOSITE: Shade has always been at a premium at the Gabba, seen here in 1962.

ABOVE: A thunderstorm approaches during day two of the fourth Test between Australia and India in January 2021. An inexperienced Indian side are about to shatter 'fortress' Gabba.

1996

Queensland looked like they were never going to win the Sheffield Shield, despite players of the quality of Wally Grout, Peter Burge, Greg Chappell and fast bowler Jeff Thomson featuring for them in the 1960s and 70s. They finally won the trophy in 1994/95 after 61 years of trying. Once the duck was broken, they have won the trophy another eight times, most recently in 2020/21.

Massive redevelopment of the ground took place between 1993 and 2005 to accommodate the local Aussie rules football side, the Brisbane Lions, and reduced capacity to 36,000. Some well-loved features, such as the fig trees and the Hill – not to be confused with South Australia's Hill but equally rowdy – have disappeared. The ground had its own Yabba (see Sydney Cricket Ground) as well, called Dancing Jack

Twoomey, a Gabba legend from the 1960s to the 1990s, who danced his way raucously round the stadium with his sombrero and his tinnies. These days, the off-field entertainment is more likely to centre round the 32,000-litre swimming pool built into the side of the grandstand with a clear screen between the pool and the outfield. The hot invitation is to watch the cricket from the Pool Deck. Come to the Gabba in your

swimming gear, wait for your photo to be taken by the Pool Deck Squad, and a dip in the pool is the reward.

Now that Brisbane has won the bid to stage the 2032 Olympics, the Queensland Government has announced that the Gabba will be the central venue used for the games, and so it will be all change again. An estimated $1 billion will be spent on demolishing the stadium's foundations and rebuilding the Gabba with new grandstands in its place, seating approximately 50,000 spectators. It will be interesting to see how cricket comes out of that upheaval.

OPPOSITE: Ian Healy of Australia leaves the field after scoring 161 not out in the first innings of the first Test against the West Indies at a distinctly low-rise Gabba, on 22nd November 1996.

RIGHT: Jackson Bird, former Olympic swimmer Stephanie Rice and cricketers Nathan Lyon and Chadd Sayers pose for the launch of the Pool Deck in 2016.

ABOVE: By the time that Steve Smith was walking off the field on 25th November 2017, having scored 141 not out, the Gabba had risen to three levels.

BELOW: These days, after another 180 years of growth, the oak is well and truly inside the boundary and the lower branches are just 22 paces from the edge of the square. If it is 450 years old, as some people say, the acorn was planted when Elizabeth I was on the throne. The tree's girth is mighty, measured at four hugs – four people linking arms can encircle it. Even a branch which fell off in a storm was turned into three seats to mark Millennium celebrations. Recognition came in 2014, when the Ickwell Oak was placed third in the Woodland Trust's Tree of the Year. In September 1989, disaster struck, as the 1953 pavilion was destroyed when fire spread through the thatched roof, leaving the building completely gutted. Fundraising events were organised and the new pavilion was opened just over a year later. In 2014, to commemorate the 175th anniversary of the first game at Ickwell, a re-enactment game took place between Ickwell and Old Warden. No doubt plenty of ladies sat or stood beneath the tree, trying to guess its age.

1926

KENSINGTON OVAL, BARBADOS
For four decades, the King never missed a big match at the Oval

ABOVE: It is likely that cricket was played in Barbados as long ago as the 1780s, although it was not till a hundred years later that Kensington Oval was founded. Home to the Pickwick Cricket Club, the playing area was originally four acres of pasture land which the club leased for a penny per annum and eventually developed into the finest ground on the island. In 1895, an English touring party under Slade Lucas, subbing for Lord Hawke, the usual leader of the touring party, took part in a remarkable five-day game. Barbados batted first and reached the unheard-of total of 517, which *The Times* reported as belonging 'more to the region of exuberant imagination that to be within the bounds of possibilities.' Unfortunately, Barbados still lost the match by 25 runs. 1910 saw a landmark moment at Kensington Oval – the first time a combined West Indies played together. The team included George Challenor, the first of the greats of West Indies cricket. His many feats included scoring 118 and 109 and taking five wickets in two matches against the MCC in 1913.

1981

ABOVE: In 1930, the Kensington Oval hosted the first-ever Test match in the West Indies, against England, with Clifford Roach scoring 122, the first Test century by a West Indian. The ground's capacity eventually reached 15,000, with new stands named after the great heroes of Barbados cricket. Among those honoured were the 3W's (Weekes, Worrell and Walcott), Sir Gary Sobers, fast bowlers Wes Hall and Charlie Griffith, and George Challenor. The ground had a resident character, the colourful King Dyal (Redvers Dundonald), who changed into a garish new suit for each session and offered his opinion from the boundary. In 2005, the ground was completely demolished, with the Pickwick Club forced to find a permanent new home. A new stadium with a capacity of 28,000 was built at a cost of $135 million in time for the 2007 World Cup. The ground also hosted the final of the 2010 ICC World T20, won by England. In the 'Now' photograph, England captain Eoin Morgan leads his team onto the field during the opening one-day match between the West Indies and England at the Kensington Oval in February 2019. The Garfield Sobers Pavilion replaced a smaller, original Garfield Sobers Pavilion and the next-door Pickwick Pavilion.

1975

LEYTON, ESSEX
Once again thriving as a centre for cricket in East London

ABOVE: Essex bought the Leyton ground as the club's headquarters in 1886 for £12,000, financed by a £10,000 mortgage. Even so, they could not afford to build a pavilion and had to launch an appeal, which raised £2,900. Over the years, Essex beat Australia, West Indies, New Zealand and Pakistan here in front of large crowds, but the ground is best remembered for the world-record stand by Yorkshire opening batsmen Percy Holmes and Herbert Sutcliffe in 1931. On the second day they reached 555, beating the previous record stand of 554. Sutcliffe then got out. Amid the celebrations, the scoreboard suddenly reverted to 554 and photographs show Holmes and Sutcliffe

shaking hands in front of a scoreboard showing 554. By evening, the score showed 555 again – the scorers had found a missing no-ball! Finances had always been difficult at Leyton and in 1933 the county moved its headquarters to Chelmsford. After the war, Essex almost gave up on Leyton and did not play there again until 1957. In the 1950s and 60s, interest in cricket revived again, but subsequently attendances dwindled. This photo from 1975 shows a John Player League match between Essex and Yorkshire, with David Bairstow behind the stumps for Yorkshire.

ABOVE: Eventually, only two first-class matches a year were played at the ground and reluctantly the county stopped playing there. Essex beat Glamorgan in the last game in August 1977. In an interview from the 2000s, Douglas Insole, Essex captain from 1950 to 1960, remembered when people queued up at 8 o'clock in the morning to get in, and recalled Leyton's moment of national prominence in 1927 when Essex vs New Zealand became the first match to be broadcast live on BBC radio. League cricket continued to be played, but it was not until 2019 that Leyton again hit the cricket headlines. Waltham Forest Council, working with the England and Wales Cricket Board, opened an Urban Cricket centre, the first of its kind in the country. The old pavilion, now a Grade II-listed building, was to be preserved. Former England captain Graham Gooch, who went to the local Gorlington School, opened the facility. Leyton once again looks to have a dynamic future, supporting youth and adult cricket in the suburbs of London. This game from 2021 features a university women's team against a local side.

1926

LORD'S

Little did Mr Henderson know that his plant nursery would become so famous

LEFT: By 1926, Lord's had existed for over 100 years, although the ground had only been owned by the MCC since 1866. Thomas Lord's first pavilion lasted for 76 years, with the odd refurbishment and expansion along the way. Eventually in 1890, it was replaced by a new pavilion designed by Thomas Verity. Lord's mainly consisted of the main grandstand, the pavilion, the Old Tavern and the Mound Stand, reputedly constructed from earth displaced by the railway construction under Wellington Road. Three-and-a-half acres of agricultural land (Henderson's Nursery) had been bought from the Clergy Orphan School in 1887 as a practice area. The ground had staged one day of first-class cricket, in 1903, when the main arena was so drenched, MCC vs Yorkshire was switched to the excellent Nursery End pitch to play a one-day match of one innings each. In 1926, after a long period of stasis, largely due to the war, Lord's was just beginning to renovate.

ABOVE: Lord's building programme for the last thirty-five years has been very progressive. Starting with the Mound Stand with its trademark canopy in 1987, the building of the dominating Media Centre in 1999, the rebuilding of the Warner Stand completed in 2017, and the completion of the new Compton and Edrich stands in 2021, redevelopment has been ceaseless. And in 2025–26, the Nursery End pitch will start to have a very different appearance. The playing area will be extended to the Wellington Road wall, in the process pulling down the Nursery Pavilion, currently a centre for hospitality and where players warm up.

Between 2003 and 2005, three of the individual stands were demolished and replaced with a single structure for the 2006 Commonwealth Games. Crowds were enormous: 93,013 attended the 2015 World Cup Final between Australia and New Zealand; 91,112 were present at the first day of the 2013 Boxing Day Ashes Test, a world record for Test cricket; and 80,883 attended a Big Bash T20 game in 2016 between the Sydney Sixers and the Perth Scorchers.

Statues of The Don, Dennis Lillee and Shane Warne are among those remembered in the G's Avenue of Legends, celebrating heroes of Australian sport.

OPPOSITE: An aerial view of the opening ceremony of the 1956 Summer Olympics at the MCG, 22nd November 1956

ABOVE: The modern MCG may have lost some of the historical elements retained by the SCG, but it is a colossal venue for cricket.

c. 1950

MEOPHAM, KENT
Once a stronghold of English cricket

ABOVE: According to its records, Meopham Cricket Club was founded in about 1776, though cricket was probably played here at least thirty years earlier. The local inn was first called The Harrow, then The Eleven Cricketers, before becoming simply The Cricketers in 1765 – the first of hundreds of pubs with that name. Overlooking the ground is the magnificent Killick's windmill constructed in 1801. Meopham cricketer Thomas Nordish was good enough to bat ahead of 'Silver Billy' Beldham in the England side in 1818. He and three other Meopham players all represented Kent, one of the strongest teams in the country.

Cricket was so central to Meopham life that a local saying was, 'to be good in Meopham you had to be good at cricket.' And, perhaps, good at lifting the elbow. Records show that in 1864, on match day, the team would have lunch in The Cricketers, down a round or two in The King's Arms after the game, and finish off the day with a 'fine old English style' dinner at The Railway Tavern. The *Daily Mirror* sent a photographer down to Kent to record a typical Saturday match for the team, with posed shots (as above) before and after the game and the obligatory old gent asleep on a pavilion bench.

c. 1950

ABOVE As William Gunyon writes in his excellent and entertaining *History of Meopham Cricket Club*, 'Meopham was the epitome of what is now the popular and romantic image of a true village team complete with squire, parson, schoolmaster, blacksmith and doctor.' Meopham won the Kent Invicta League five times between 1994 and 2007, then moved to the Kent County Village League, which they won in 2014. Because the Green is not the largest of playing areas, T20 has been banned for fear of causing collateral damage to cars (there is also the busy main road that runs along one side of the green). Sadly, the club suffered from vandalism in 2018, which caused significant damage to the ground, and home games had to be played away in 2019. Once, portraits of bewhiskered heroes of the past featured on the pub sign of The Cricketers, but now the sign depicts bat, ball, windmill and tankard.

c. 1897

MERION, PHILADELPHIA

Home to one of the East Coast's most historic clubs

ABOVE: Merion Cricket Club was founded in 1865 by fifteen young enthusiasts who played on Colonel Owen Jones's estate in Wynnewood in the suburbs of Philadelphia. By 1892, the club had moved to Haverford, also in Philadelphia, and become one of the big four teams from which the Gentlemen of Philadelphia sides were selected. Merion hosted touring parties such as Lord Hawke's 1894 England XI, the 1896 Australian touring party and Sir Pelham Warner's XI in 1897. Gilbert Jessop played for Warner's team, and the combined side included J.B. King, probably the greatest cricketer produced by North America. Merion did not have much luck with their clubhouses or Main House, as they were called. Three burnt down in the space of four years out of six constructed at various sites. The sixth, built at Merion in 1896 and described as 'the most complete and largest country-club house in this country', had both gas and electric lights, library, bedrooms and a large theatre. Built of stone and brick, it proved fireproof.

RIGHT: Undoubtedly, Philadelphia's John 'Bart' King can claim the outstanding performance at Merion. Bowling was his main strength but on this occasion it was his batting which excelled. His 344 not out for Belmont against Merion in 1906 is still the highest score ever made in North America. But cricket was becoming a niche activity, not helped by the Imperial Cricket Conference, which allowed only countries within the British Empire to play each other internationally. By the beginning of the 20th century, Merion had expanded into other sports, particularly tennis on the Great Lawn (a similar arrangement to Aigburth in Liverpool), squash and two golf courses, though still under the name of the cricket club. Although the game of cricket had dwindled to nothing by the 1920s, it was reintroduced in 1972. The club was designated a National Historic Landmark in 1987 for its leading role in the promotion, development and continued support of cricket, golf, squash and tennis in the United States.

has the largest fixed seating capacity outside Test match arenas in the whole of the country. Despite that, the open stands and lack of fencing give the arena an informal feel which makes the spectator feel included in the action. The pitch is one of the quickest in the area, and in 2014 the groundsman John Dodds completed a hat-trick when he was named ECB Groundsman of the Year for the third time in a row. That followed the *Guardian* naming North Marine Road 'Ground of the Year' in 2010.

Of all the outgrounds where Yorkshire once played – Sheffield, Bradford, Middlesborough and half a dozen others – only Scarborough remains, a sign of the seaside resort's popularity and commercial success. Excluding Test venues, North Marine Road might well be the best-supported ground in the country, attracting five or six thousand a day. Recognising this, Yorkshire have signed a new 10-year agreement with the club. Unfortunately, the 2020 Festival was cancelled due to the pandemic, the first time this had happened outside wartime. To compensate, Yorkshire were set to play Lancashire at Scarborough in 2021, but social distancing meant that the expected full house would have been reduced by an uneconomic three-quarters. The game was transferred to Headingley, although the Roses match was rescheduled for 2022. 'First-class cricket on holiday', the *Yorkshire Post*'s old cricket correspondent J.M. Kilburn called cricket at Scarborough.

1897

2924. THE GRANDSTAND.

SYDNEY CRICKET GROUND

SCG has maintained a link to the past with the preservation of its two historic pavilions

Like most modern Australian stadia, the SCG is used for a variety of sports, including cricket, football, cycling and biking. In the past, crowds have reached 78,000 for rugby league, but today, the capacity of the all-seater stadium is nearer 46,000.

The SCG began life as the Garrison Ground under the control of the British military and it was British soldiers who took part in the earliest recorded match

in 1854. When the space was turned into public gardens, sports activities moved to another part of Sydney Common, named Moore Park after the Mayor of Sydney, Charles Moore. Advised by the Director of the Royal Botanical Gardens, confusingly also called Charles Moore, the mayor planted a number of Moreton Bay Fig trees which are still going strong.

Just as confusingly, the ground underwent several

OPPOSITE: The 1897 photograph shows the Members' Pavilion (nearest) with the Ladies' Pavilion in the background. Encircling the ground and opened the same day as the Ladies' Pavilion, is a cycling track, which George Bradman, the Don's father, helped to build.

ABOVE: Little has changed in over a century... apart from the price of membership, which is now eye-watering.

c. 1900

name changes before the NSW Association assumed control in 1875 of what was now known as the Association Ground. The first game was between civil service teams, which may sound prosaic, but the sides included Dave Gregory, Australia's first-ever Test captain, Alick Bannerman, who also played for Australia, and other good-quality players.

In the first Sydney Test match in 1882, Australia beat England by five wickets. By then, the ground was well-provided with stands including the Old Members' Pavilion and the Brewongle Stand. Test matches were exclusively between England and Australia to the end of the century, shaded by the Australians eight to six with no draws. In 1892, Lord Sheffield's XI, captained by W.G. Grace, lost to an Australian XI at the ground. Lord Sheffield still donated £150 for the establishment of a competition to be called The Sheffield Shield. Finally, in

1894, the venue was conclusively renamed the Sydney Cricket Ground.

As the size of crowds increased, further stands were constructed or replaced in rapid succession. The Members' Pavilion was built in 1886 and the stylish green-roofed Ladies' Pavilion opened in 1896. Both are heritage-listed and very fine examples of their type. The 'Bob' stand, built in 1895 and now relocated to the

ABOVE: Horse-drawn coaches arrive at the rear of the Lady Members' Stand. The foundation stone was set in 1896 by Viscountess Hampden, wife of the then NSW Governor. The completed stand was opened later that year.

RIGHT: A pre-war aerial photo of the SCG, showing the rear of both members' pavilions, the wide open space of the Hill and also the Sydney Showground beyond.

1936

North Sydney Oval, got its nickname in the Depression era because it cost 1 shilling (a bob) to get in. The first mechanical scoreboard, erected in 1896, was regarded as a great advance and survived until 1924. The famous Robertson and Martin-designed scoreboard which replaced it remained in operation for almost 60 years.

The Bradman Stand was constructed in 1974 and honoured the man who had drawn large crowds to the stadium, albeit he transferred his allegiance to South Australia in 1934. Nighttime cricket became popular and two huge stands and six light towers were erected in 1978 to take advantage of this new audience. Three new stands were built in 2014 at a cost of $197.5 million. One of them, the Victor Trumper stand, occupies what was once the famous Hill, where Yabba thrived, the best known of all barrackers. A sample, to English captain Douglas Jardine in the Bodyline series: 'Leave our flies alone, Jardine – they're the only friends you've got here!' A sculpture of Yabba in characteristic barracking pose was allocated a seat in the stand. More recently, stands full of spectators have been known to don their trademark Richie Benaud outfits: silver-haired wig, white blazer, club tie and, most importantly, Channel 9 microphone, in affectionate memory of the former captain of Australia and New South Wales. Benaud is also one of the sport's sculptures forming part of the ground's tribute to NSW sportsmen and women, which include Fred Spofforth and Steve Waugh. There is also a plaque which remembers Philip Hughes, who died during a

TAUNTON, SOMERSET
The perfect ground for a one-day game

LEFT: Of all the first-class counties, only one was founded outside its own borders. Somerset was formed in 1875 at Sidmouth, a good twenty miles into Devon, after a match between the Gentlemen of Somerset and their Devon equivalents. Initially Somerset was a nomadic team which played its games around the county, but in 1881 they settled in Priory Fields, Taunton, beside the River Tone, purchasing the ground in 1896. The Australians were early visitors in 1882 with Spofforth taking 13 wickets in an easy victory. After winning 12 out of 13 games in 1890, the county joined the championship in 1891 and in 1892 finished third, which they did not equal until 1958. Nevertheless, they were not recognised as a 'first-class' team until 1895. Famous names who played for Somerset include Australian Bill Alley, the last batsman to score three thousand runs in a season. Despite these and many other fine players, Somerset failed to win any trophies. Here, spectators watch the Gillette Cup semi-final against Lancashire in July 1970. Lancashire won by four wickets.

ABOVE: The club finally won its first trophies – the Gillette Cup and the John Player League – under Brian Rose in 1979. In recent years, a building boom has totally changed the cricket ground, although St James' Church beyond remains the same. The striking New Somerset Pavilion was designed by LED Architects and replaced the two previous grandstands. It provides seating for approximately 1,200 spectators over three floors, including 344 seats at roof level. The Colin Atkinson Pavilion, which had been around since the 1970s, was totally gutted and refurbished and there is a new pavilion for the players – the £3.8 million Andy Caddick Pavilion, named after a very fine fast bowler for England. The ground – known as The Cooper Associates County Ground – is aiming for a capacity of 15,000 and has already hosted a women's international T20 game between England and New Zealand. Taunton is an exciting place to watch one-day games and is the highest scoring T20 ground in the world. The County Championship still eludes Somerset, though they came desperately close in 2019, beaten by Essex.

TILFORD, SURREY

An archetypal village cricket green, with a far-from-typical pavilion

BELOW: Officially, Tilford CC was founded in 1885, but locals – citing *Wisden* – insist that cricket has been played on the Green 'longer than anywhere except Hambledon', although Sevenoaks Vine and Mitcham Green might argue the point. It's the home ground of 'Silver Billy' Beldham (1766–1862), one of the greatest batsmen of the underarm era. A local boy from nearby Wrecclesham, after his cricket career was over he retired to Tilford as landlord of The Barley Mow in 1822 and lived there till his death. Across the Green (and uphill) is the Tilford Institute designed by Sir Edward Lutyens in 1894, which is both a community hall and acts as the club's pavilion. In 1904, Tilford joined the l'Anson League, reputedly the oldest continuously operating village cricket league in the country, and won a hat-trick of titles from 1908–10. In 1936, when a Tilford game was broadcast in tandem with a Test match, the commentator, Lieutenant Commander Woodrooffe of 'The fleet's lit up!' fame, remarked 'This is cricket as it should be played. The game started like this on the village green... I would rather be here than at the Test match in Manchester.'

1971

BELOW: Nothing very much changes at Tilford. The Barley Mow is recognisably the same as 150 years ago and was voted Best Surrey Pub in 2018, so keeps up a good standard. You won't find as many cars on the outfield as in 1971 – and certainly no Austin A38s – because parking is not encouraged. The club celebrated its centenary in 1985 with a visit from a Surrey side which included Alec Stewart, Monte Lynch, Pat Pocock and Mark Butcher. As part of Pat Pocock's Benefit Year activities, Sir Ernest Harrison offered to pay £50 into the testimonial funds if Monte Lynch hit the ball for six with a bat in one hand and an ice cream in the other… The club plays in the first division of the I'Anson League, which they won in 2014 and again in 2021. The team is virtually all locals and this, says chairman Nigel Martyn, 'makes it all the more satisfying'. Meantime, for those of a fanciful nature, beware of the pub on a dark evening – the ghost of Silver Billy is said to haunt the place.

RIGHT: Cricketers walk back to the field of play after the tea interval from the Tilford Institute building. Tilford Green is long and narrow, so the square is more of a rectangle, with two rows of wickets.

129

c. 1939

2017

TRENT BRIDGE
One of the more intimate English Test venues

Before the County Championship was formalised in 1890, the press used to vote for the winners of an unofficial championship. Gloucestershire, with the three Grace brothers, and Yorkshire won several titles, but Nottinghamshire, with more than twenty won or shared, were way out ahead. George Parr,

known as the Lion of the North, was the first of their great players in the 1850s.

The county played first at council-owned The Forest, where they were not allowed to charge entrance fees, so in 1838 they moved to Trent Bridge on the initiative of William Clarke, later to captain the All-England XI. An

OPPOSITE: An aerial view of the ground with a full house c. 1939. In those days you could get a good view of the pitch from the Trent Bridge Inn at the centre top of the picture.

ABOVE: Building work continues on the giant Radcliffe Road Stand before the start of the 2017 season.

OTHER CRICKET TITLES

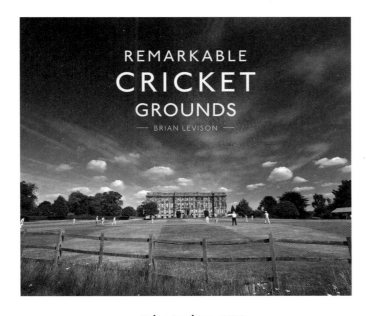

Brian Levison, 2016
978-1-911216-05-6 • 224 pages • Hardback
UK £25
* Shortlisted for Sports Book of the Year

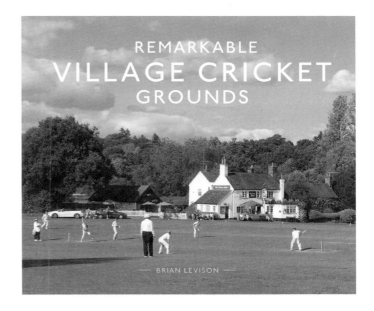

Brian Levison, 2018
978-1-911595-56-4 • 224 pages • Hardback
UK £25

Featuring: Adelaide Oval, Ageas Bowl, Arnos Vale Stadium, Bamburgh Castle, Basin Reserve, Blenheim Palace, Blundstone Arena, Boland Bank Park, Bournville, Bridgetown Cricket Ground, Broadhalfpenny Down, Castle Ashby House, Chail Cricket Ground, Charters Towers Goldfield, Cheltenham College, Citi Field, City Oval, Clifton County Cricket Club, Coniston Cricket Ground, Crooklets Cricket Ground, Darren Sammy National Cricket Ground, Dubai International Cricket Stadium, Eden Gardens, Emirates Old Trafford, Etihad Stadium/Melbourne, Feroz Shah Kotla Ground, Fitz Park, The Gabba, Galle International Stadium, The Grange, Hagley Oval, Headingley Carnegie Stadium, Himachal Pradesh Cricket Association (HPCA) Stadium, Jawaharlal Nehru International Stadium, Kapiolani Park, Kia Oval, Lake St. Moritz, Laurie Lee Field, Lord Braybrooke's Ground, Lord's, M.A. Chidambaram Stadium, Maifeld, Melbourne Cricket Ground, Milton Abbey School, Mitcham Cricket Green, Moses Mabhida Stadium, Narol Cricket Stadium, New Field, New Road, New Williamfield, Newlands Cricket Grounds, North Marine Road Ground, Oval Maidan, Padang Field, The Parks, Penrhos Estate, Portchester Castle, Pukekura Park, Queenstown Events Centre, Raby Castle, Sheikh Zayed Cricket Stadium, The Ship Inn, Sir Paul Getty's Ground, Spianada Square, Spitfire Ground, Spotless Stadium, Spout House, St. Peter's Cricket Club, Stanford Cricket Ground, Stoneleigh Abbey, Surnikovo Cricket Ground, Sydney Cricket Ground, Valley of the Rocks, Vincent Square, Wankhede Stadium, Whitbread Estate, Yeonhui Cricket Stadium.

Featuring: Abbotsbury, Abinger Hammer, Alderley Edge, Ambleside, Arthington, Audley End, Bamburgh, Bearsted, Belvoir Castle, Benenden Green, Bilsington, Blenheim Palace, Booth, Bridgetown, Bude, Burnsall, Castleton, Chagford, Cholmondeley Castle, Clanfield, Clumber Park, Cockington, Coldharbour, Coniston, Copley, Cowdray Park, Crickhowell, Doo'cot Park, Dumbleton, Ebernoe, Elmley Castle, Firle, Fulking, Goodwood, Grassington, Great Budworth, Hagley Hall, Haworth, Holkham Hall, Honley, Hovingham, Ickwell, Instow, Keswick, Kildale, Kinross, Knightshayes Court, Knole Park, Leigh, Linkenholt, Longparish, Luddenfoot, Lurgashall, Lustleigh, Lyndhurst, Marchwiel, Menai Bridge, Meopham, Mountnessing, Mytholmroyd, North Nibley, Northop, Old Town, Oxted, Patterdale, Penshurst Place, Raby Castle, Ramsbottom, Rawtenstall, Saltaire, Sedgewick, Sheepscombe, Shobrooke Park, Sicklinghall, Sidmouth, Snettisham, Southborough, Southill Park, Spout House, Stanton, Stanway, Stoneleigh, Tilford, Triangle, Ullenwood, Uplyme, Valley of the Rocks, Warborough, Warkworth Castle, White Coppice, Wingfield, Winnington Park.